Promoting Reading for Pleasure in the Primary School

Michael Lockwood

Los Angeles • London • New Delhi • Singapore

First published 2008

SAGE Publications Ltd
1 Oliver's Yard
55 City Road
London EC1Y 1SP

SAGE Publications Inc.
2455 Teller Road
Thousand Oaks, California 91320

SAGE Publications India Pvt Ltd
B 1/I 1 Mohan Cooperative Industrial Area
Mathura Road
New Delhi 110 044

SAGE Publications Asia-Pacific Pte Ltd
33 Pekin Street #02-01
Far East Square
Singapore 048763

Library of Congress Control Number: 2007942816

British Library Cataloguing in Publication data

A catalogue record for this book is available
from the British Library

ISBN 978-1-4129-2966-0
ISBN 978-1-4129-2967-7 (pbk)

Typeset by C&M Digitals (P) Ltd, Chennai, India
Printed in Great Britain by Cromwell Press Ltd, Trowbridge, Wiltshire
Printed on paper from sustainable resources

To my fellow flood-survivors, Kate, Amy and Grace – with love

Contents

Acknowledgements

I would like to thank most sincerely all those children, parents and teachers who have contributed to my project.

In particular, I am really grateful to the following English subject leaders for sharing their time, thoughts and ideas with me, usually at the end of a very busy day. Please take a bow:

Carolyn Ripper, Clare Wapshare, Elen Peale, Gill Clark, Helen Blumfield, Jacky Steele, Jenny Hill, Jill Hanson, Jill Woof, Martin Gater, Melissa Cliffe, Rachel Crystal, Rachel Pickup, Rosemary Edwards, Sarah Bergson, Sue Masters and Wendy Long.

Special thanks also to Reetinder Boparai for being such an able and interested research officer and to Dr Margaret Perkins for collaboration in the early stages of the project.

Finally, I would like to thank the British Academy for the funding which allowed me to undertake the research that lies behind this book and also Philip Pullman and Mary Sutcliffe for generously supporting the original funding application.

Preface

I do not remember the teachers who taught me to read or the first book I read unaided. In fact, I remember no books at all from my primary school, though books of some sort there must have been. I also have no memory of being read to at home, though I'm sure this must have happened.

What I do remember, though, is the first library I belonged to and the books I first borrowed from there. It was a small branch library located on a parade of shops on the Bradford council estate where we were living at the time. I ought to thank the enlightened councillors who decided to put it there. It had large plate glass windows, wooden shelving and librarians who kept a stern eye on your behaviour: 'Would you do that at home?' they would ask, if you treated the books roughly. The answer I was too scared to give was that we had no books at home, apart from my mother's Agatha Christie collection in a corner bookcase. I remember going to this library with my sisters when I was about 9 or 10 and borrowing the *Corrigan* adventure series by R.B. Maddox, the *Biggles* books by W.E. Johns and Enid Blyton's *Famous Five*. These were books *I* chose: the librarians, whatever they thought of my choices, made no comment. I consumed them avidly, in great quantities and with simple pleasure, and the imaginative world of these adventure stories fed into the games I played. Later, at the start of secondary school, I wrote a book review of a *Biggles* novel and can remember my English teacher's icy comment: 'Are you *still* reading those, Lockwood?' That particular seam of pleasure reading was from that moment closed off as I started on the study of 'English Literature'. I carried on reading comics and annuals, though, such as *Tiger* and *Roy of the Rovers*, with the same enjoyment, and devoured my dad's *Daily Mirror* when he came home from his night shift and we passed briefly at breakfast time. I would read this, starting with the back pages where the sports section was, and work my way towards the front, a habit I still have today. However, I would no more have mentioned this leisure reading to my teachers than I would have invited them home for afternoon tea. School and home reading were two separate planets on orbits that could never meet. I did not think that what I was doing even counted as reading: it was more like a bad habit or a way of wasting time better spent on something else.

When I look back, I see that popular series fiction, comics and newspapers were where I got the pleasure reading habit, not from school. From school I got a feeling of guilt about my home reading, a feeling that I ought to be reading something more improving or serious. As the study of 'Literature' gradually took over, I cultivated a different sort of appreciation for some of the books we studied, an enjoyment of a different kind, more complex, subtle and reflective and bound up with essays and exams. It wasn't until I became a middle school teacher myself and then later a parent, and rediscovered children's books, that the simple joys of reading I experienced with my first library books returned, unalloyed by guilt: it was all right to read these books because it was part of my job or my parental role.

Action Point

Jot down some notes for your own reading autobiography. What texts did you read for pleasure up to the age of 11? Were they ones that you read at home or at school? Were they texts that were read aloud to you or did you read them yourself? Did your parents/teachers approve of them? What influence did this early reading have on you?

I went back to look at my old council house and the local library a few years ago. Both were empty, boarded up and in disrepair. For the children of that community today, the local school is now the place where they will need to develop the pleasure reading habit, if it is not part of their home life. I have written this book to try to suggest ways in which all primary schools, whether on council estates or in leafy suburbs, can help young readers today discover enjoyment in reading within the school and the classroom, and make links between home and school reading so that each nourishes the other.

This book has been informed by a research project in the area of promoting reading for enjoyment, funded by the British Academy. The aim of this research was very straightforward: to identify primary schools and teachers who have demonstrated good practice in the area of promoting the pleasures of reading and to disseminate what seems transferable from these good schools to other schools who want to improve their practice.

Over a two-year period, from 2005 to 2007, I used written questionnaires to survey the views of teachers, children and parents. I began by writing to a sample of 100 primary schools within a region in the south-east of England to find out about school policy and practice with regard to promoting reading for pleasure and positive attitudes to reading. I eventually received responses from teachers in 40 of the schools, drawn from nine different local authorities. These volunteer schools were clearly a self-selecting group of enthusiasts, as their responses to my questionnaire made clear. I carried out reading surveys with over 1,400 of their Year 5 (9–10-year-old) pupils, eliciting their

views on reading and on themselves as readers. I also sent further questionnaires to parents of these pupils, then in Year 6, and received over 300 replies.
The results of the pupil reading surveys led me to identify a smaller group of
schools which were clearly having particular success in motivating their
pupils to read for enjoyment. I visited each of these schools to interview the
English subject leaders at length about the strategies they had used to promote reading so effectively with their pupils.

I have used the quantitative and qualitative data from these questionnaires
and interviews throughout this book to support and illustrate the points
I make. In particular, I have provided regular case studies of schools where
I found examples of good planning and good practice that had been shown
to work. I have also deliberately let the children's voices be heard, as well as
those of teachers and parents, since they are often ignored in debates about
reading, and important lessons can be learnt from them. Where the children's
words are used, spelling, punctuation and grammar have been silently cor-
rected when necessary, since it is what they have to say which is important
rather than presentational features.

However, the book is not an academic account of my research project: that
would not be appropriate here. It takes a wider brief. It is an attempt to make
what I have found out from my research and related background reading,
along with my own ideas, available and accessible to a wider audience of
interested professionals; to try to translate research findings into a more practical form that can help spread successful practice in promoting reading
for pleasure.

Lessons from the children

At the end of the multiple choice Reading Surveys I carried out with primary pupils, I
asked them to write or draw anything else they would like to say about reading, in the
box that was provided. This qualitative data, both words and drawings, proved just as
interesting as the quantitative data, the numbers, mentioned throughout the chapters
that follow.

The first lesson from the children who responded was an important one: there is more
to life than reading and certainly more to childhood than books! These pleasures have
their place and time, in the classroom, library and at home, but out in the playground
there are other, more serious matters to attend to. In response to two questions in my
Reading Survey which asked what your 'best friends' think about reading, one child wrote
a scathing reply (see Figure 1).

> Please write or draw anything else you would like to say about reading in this box.
>
> I think question
> 1st are extremly daft
> questions This is because
> I do not talk about
> such trivial matters outside in
> the Playground.

Figure 1.1　*One child's response to a question about friends' attitudes to reading*

Chapter 1

Introduction

Summary

Chapter 1 defines the term 'reading for pleasure' and related terminology, and looks briefly at the history of reading for pleasure. It then explores the background to the current concern about children's attitudes to reading resulting from the PISA and PIRLS international surveys, along with the official government responses and initiatives which followed, such as Reading Connects and the National Year of Reading. The chapter also considers the evidence from national and international research in the area of reading engagement and motivation, and from previous surveys of British children's reading attitudes.

Reading for Pleasure

This book takes as its subject the promotion of 'reading for pleasure'. I chose this term because, along with 'reading for enjoyment', it is the one used most often in official British curriculum documents. 'Pleasure' and 'enjoyment' are both words that occur, for example, in England's National Curriculum (NC) programmes of study for reading (DfEE/QCA, 1999: 46). Within reading for pleasure, I include the reading of popular as well as literary fiction, of comics and magazines as well as books, non-fiction as well as fiction, and electronic as well as printed texts. Reading for pleasure can take place in or out of the school, at home, in the public library or indeed anywhere, and often involves what is called 'wider reading' or 'independent reading'. Related terms used in the United States are 'free voluntary reading' and 'recreational reading'. Reading for pleasure is one very important and common manifestation of having a positive 'attitude to reading', which is another term frequently used in the research and writing in this area. Having a positive attitude to reading is obviously closely related to the concepts of 'reading engagement' and 'reading motivation', which link to a much wider literature on learning motivation generally. 'Reluctance to read' is a term most often used in British education to describe readers who do not take pleasure in reading and avoid it if they can.

Reading for pleasure has not always been seen as a good thing, particularly reading fiction for pleasure. This is difficult to grasp at a time when the leisure reading of fiction by adults and especially children meets with general approval, and when reading groups and television book shows are more popular than ever. However, novel reading was widely seen as frivolous and a waste of time when the genre first appeared in the seventeenth and eighteenth centuries. The term 'novel' itself suggested something slight and ephemeral, trading on its 'novelty value' and giving instant gratification; metaphors of drug-taking and addiction or over-indulgence were commonly applied to its effects. At that time, the new genre was firmly part of popular rather than literary culture and its readers were looked down upon by the cultural elite. When the novel later achieved the status of literature worthy of attention by educated readers, there was still a clear divide between popular fiction, seen as sensationalist and a bad influence on its susceptible readers, and 'serious' literary fiction, seen as morally improving and aesthetically pleasing. This divide remains today in the attitude we take to different forms of reading for pleasure: we are likely to be much more disapproving of the Mills & Boon reader than of the reader of Jane Austen and the Brontës, although the reading experience may be equally enjoyable for the readers concerned. Also today, of course, we are ambivalent about the enjoyment of other popular cultural forms of reading, particularly ones involving young people, such as teenage magazines, graphic novels and all forms of electronic texts.

Victor Nell, in *Lost In a Book: The Psychology of Reading for Pleasure,* traces this prejudice against the pleasure principle back to the Protestant work ethic and further back to restraints on storytelling in earlier cultures. He sees teachers and librarians, the gatekeepers of literary culture, as having been important figures in our society in counteracting the 'noxious influence' of popular fiction, seen as the 'plague of the spirit, death of the mind' (Nell, 1988: 26). Nell describes as an 'elitist fallacy' the idea that as readers become more sophisticated they leave this 'trash' behind (Nell, 1988: 4). The early public libraries, certainly, saw their role as providing information rather than entertainment to their members; fiction-lending generally was treated with suspicion and had strict limits. Even when public libraries bowed to the demands of readers and freely lent fiction, they were still reluctant to stock anything other than literary texts and adult-approved classics for children, rather than say popular series fiction. Fortunately for me, this had changed by the time I joined my local library in the 1960s. Even today when two-thirds of adult borrowing is fiction and the emphasis in reader advisory services is put 'not on the quality of the book, but on the quality of the reading experience, as determined by the reader' (Ross et al., 2006: 213), there is still debate about to what extent libraries should be in the entertainment rather than the education business, particularly when it comes to children's collections.

Teachers, of course, have always been in the education business and historically have seen their role as teaching children to read, even if the children did not necessarily enjoy the experience. Metaphors of reading as a ladder or a key, rather than as food or a drug, were more likely to be used here (Ross et al., 2006: 16). Reading was a necessary skill to climb the rungs of the school curriculum, or to unlock the doors of knowledge in other subjects; a means to an end rather than an end in itself. For this purpose texts were chosen to help develop reading skills and then promote social and moral improvement, or the training of aesthetic sensibility, rather than to entertain. Nell (1988: 40) sees the development of reader-oriented approaches to literary studies in more recent years as putting power in readers' hands, rather than 'expert' critics and teachers. However, teachers today still feel ambivalent about handing critical power over to their pupils and are often unsure about using popular forms of both fiction and non-fiction which they know children enjoy out of school.

Pause for Thought

Reading has been compared at different times to a ladder, a key, a tool, an addictive drug, an infectious bug, a magic carpet and so on. What metaphor would you use to characterise the activity? Would you use a different metaphor for different aspects of reading?

The Current Context

In June 2006 the Queen hosted a party to celebrate British children's literature, at the end of which she said to the assembled audience:

> British children's literature has been for many years an extraordinary success story and I am glad we have been able to celebrate this great achievement here at Buckingham Palace. We have been reminded that this magic of our childhoods … is an enduring and essential part of our culture … and I hope that this event will encourage you … to read some of the wonderful books from which the characters came and to discover the pleasure of reading.

Also in that year, Gordon Brown, then Chancellor and later Prime Minister, and an avid reader himself, asked the literacy charity Booktrust to host his children's Christmas party on the theme of reading for pleasure, and to design the Treasury Christmas card. The official seal of approval was thus given to attempts to nurture the pleasure reading habit in British children. These were two high-profile manifestations of a movement to reinstate the pleasure principle in children's reading which has gathered momentum in the United Kingdom since 2001. It has been a movement generated by cultural anxiety, a bout of moral panic born out of mounting evidence that in fact British children no longer *did* enjoy reading, even though they were better at it than ever before and better than many other children around the world. For many teachers, consultants and researchers this movement was a vindication of what they had continued to say and do throughout the years when 'fun' was not a word that was associated with reading or the teaching of reading.

Doubts were first raised by a number of well-publicised surveys, beginning with the Programme for International Student Assessment (PISA) study of 15-year-olds' reading which was conducted in 2000. *Reading for Change: Results from PISA 2000*, an analysis of the overall results of this major study, reached two particularly startling conclusions:

- Being more enthusiastic about reading and being a frequent reader was more of an advantage on its own than having well-educated parents in good jobs.
- Finding ways to engage students in reading may be one of the most effective ways to leverage social change.
  (Organisation for Economic Co-operation and Development [OECD], 2002: 3)

Here was evidence from a large-scale, scientific study that not only was the enjoyment of reading good for children because it was enjoyable, but also because it had the potential to overcome social disadvantage, which has been an aim of liberal education policy in Britain since at least 1870. Looking back at my reading autobiography, this was certainly the case for me.

The aptly titled *Reading for Change* also concluded that: 'cognitive skills and reading motivation are mutually reinforcing ... rather than being alternatives, schools need to address both simultaneously' (OECD, 2002). The evidence showed that the 'will' to read needed to be developed alongside the 'skill' to read because each feeds the other. Given these conclusions, there was disappointment to discover that 15-year-olds in the United Kingdom were below the OECD average when it came to 'engagement in reading', ranking 20th out of 27 countries. 'Engagement' here included reading for pleasure, reading widely and attitude to reading. This was more surprising when another table of the same countries showed UK pupils actually came first in terms of 'engagement at school' considered more generally. The PISA survey is repeated every three years, but unfortunately the United Kingdom was not able to enter a large enough sample to be part of the official results for PISA 2003 (anecdotally, because UK secondary schools felt their pupils already had too many assessments).

The following year, 2001, the Progress in International Reading Literacy Study of 150,000 9–10-year-olds in 35 countries (PIRLS) was carried out. Again there was a stark contrast in the findings, this time confined to pupils in England. It reported that English pupils came joint first in terms of attainment in reading for literary purposes, although the validity of this finding has been challenged

(Hilton, 2007). However, the same pupils were placed 27th in terms of attitudes toward reading, well below the international average (International Association for the Evaluation of Educational Achievement, 2001).

For a government that had used league tables as instruments to bring about educational change, there was potential for embarrassment here. The plus points of PISA and PIRLS were duly celebrated as confirmation that government policy had driven up reading attainment standards, and evidence from PIRLS that England also had 'a long tail of underachievement' in reading attainment was simply seen as evidence that a further drive was still needed. However, the suggestion from the PIRLS analysis that, in ratcheting up reading attainment, the government had in the process damaged reading engagement could not be ignored.

The pressure to do something about this was increased when a group of well-known British children's authors, including Bernard Ashley, Philip Pullman, Anne Fine, Jamila Gavin and Chris Powling, lobbied government ministers to highlight the problem. Philip Pullman summed up the disquiet the authors felt:

> I am concerned that in a constant search for things to test, we're forgetting the true purpose, the true nature, of reading and writing; and in forcing these things to happen in a way that divorces them from pleasure, we are creating a generation of children who might be able to make the right noises when they see print, but who hate reading and feel nothing but hostility for literature. (Powling et al., 2003: 10)

A second book two years later added the names of Quentin Blake, Michael Morpurgo, Alison Prince, Michael Rosen and Jacqueline Wilson to the lobbyists. The finger of blame for the concerns the authors had about the teaching of reading was firmly pointed at the central plank of the UK government's project for raising standards, the National Literacy Strategy (NLS), introduced in 1998. The authors highlighted 'the damage the [National Literacy] strategy was doing to children's reading and writing for pleasure' by its narrow focus on genre characteristics, word and sentence level features, and decontextualised extracts from books (Ashley et al., 2005: 5).

Librarians made a similar diagnosis of the problem. Judith Elkin commented:

> There is an interesting, and apparently increasing, dichotomy between the teaching of reading in school and reading for pleasure ... It is vital that the concept of reading for pleasure is encouraged in schools. There has been concern, recently, that government initiatives such as the NLS are squeezing out the fun aspect of reading and that there is little room to promote the concept of reading for pleasure, reading for its own sake. (Elkin et al., 2003: 76)

These comments tended to confirm predictions made by some at the time of the introduction of the NLS. For example, in a volume published in 1998, *Literacy Is Not Enough: Essays on the Importance of Reading,* distinguished contributors from a variety of fields such as Brian Cox, author of the first NC, Eric Bolton, former Chief Inspector of Schools for England and Wales, the novelist Doris Lessing, academics Henrietta Dombey and Margaret Meek, and the politician Roy Hattersley, warned of the dangers that a more functional, instrumental approach to teaching reading, which put the stress on 'literacy' rather than literature, could bring: 'Literacy is a necessity: reading is (or ought to be) the most universal and easily accessible of pleasures' (Cox, 1998: 50).

More publicity was given to another royal contribution to the debate when the Prince of Wales's Arts and Kids Foundation made headlines with a survey in 2004 which found that 24% of boys and 16% of girls aged 7–14 could not name a favourite book unprompted (*TES*, 2004). Concern was shifting towards what Nicole Irwin has called '"aliteracy": the lack of a reading habit in capable readers who choose not to read' (Irwin, 2003: 29).

Other independent surveys of children's reading habits found evidence to back up this concern. The NFER Reading Attitudes Survey, carried out in 1998 and again in 2003 with Year 4 (8–9 years) and Year 6 (10–11 years) samples, confirmed the PIRLS findings. It concluded that English pupils were good at reading, and this was reflected in their confidence as readers; however, their enjoyment of reading was poor compared with other countries and had declined over recent years. The report again suggested a connection with the introduction of the NLS:

> Children are less likely to find reading difficult and to need support. They are also less likely to enjoy reading … there is some evidence, though far from conclusive, that the very strategy that has improved children's ability and confidence has also made them less likely to read for pleasure. (Sainsbury and Schagen, 2004: 385)

Naomi Dungworth and others (2004) surveyed the reading habits of 132 Year 5 (9–10 years) pupils and found that 50% of boys enjoyed reading only 'a little' and only 50% of children read at home each day. Their conclusion again was that the promotion of reading for pleasure in the school curriculum should be a priority.

Finally, the most recent survey, the National Literacy Trust's *Children's and Young People's Reading Habits and Preferences* (2005) was more determinedly upbeat in the interpretation of its findings, concluding that the majority of pupils held positive attitudes towards reading, which is the finding of most surveys of British primary school pupils. However, this still meant that only just over half the sample said they enjoyed reading either 'very much' or 'quite a lot' and the majority of boys enjoyed reading only 'a bit' or 'not at all'.

Contrast this, though, with a survey carried out in 1994, before the introduction of the NLS. Hall and Coles (1999) looked at *Children's Reading Choices* and concluded not only that voluntary reading 'remains a very significant leisure time activity for children' (p. 1), and compared with a similar 1977 survey had increased significantly for both 10-year-old boys and girls, but also that 77% of 10-year-olds had positive attitudes to reading.

> ### Action Point
>
> Carry out a survey of children's reading in a school or other setting. The survey could cover tastes and preferences, attitudes, views about reading and/or self-concept as a reader. The National Literacy Trust's 2005 survey is a wide-ranging one and the questionnaire used is available online (www.literacytrust.org.uk).

The five-yearly PIRLS survey was carried out again in May–June 2006, involving 150 English primary schools and 4,000 pupils, and the results, reported in November 2007, were even more disappointing, provoking an editorial in the *Times Educational Supplement* with the headline: 'Let's put the joy back into reading' (*TES*, 2007). In terms of attitudes to reading, English 9–10-year-olds were still well below the international average in PIRLS 2006 and were now ranked 37th out of the 45 countries or provinces taking part. This was in fact a significant worsening of the situation found in 2001, with 15% of English pupils now having an unfavourable attitude to reading, almost double the international average. The lack of enjoyment in reading by this sizeable minority was not confined to schools: a table concerned with 'Reading for Fun Outside of School' placed England 38th out of the 45 participants. There was also a significant downward trend in achievement in reading, both for literary and informational purposes (http://pirls.bc.edu/pirls2006/intlr_pt.html). The PISA 2006 survey, published in December 2007, (OECD, 2007) also showed a decline in the reading performance of UK 15-year-olds relative to other countries since the previous study in 2000 (www.pisa.oecd.org).

Official Responses

In 2003 the word 'fun' made a rare appearance in an official UK curriculum document. This was *Excellence and Enjoyment: A Strategy for Primary Schools*, which set out the following aims in response to criticism of the rigidity and narrowness of a primary curriculum dominated by the literacy and numeracy strategies:

> We want schools to continue to focus on raising standards while not being afraid to combine that with making learning fun. Our goal is for every primary school to combine excellence in teaching with enjoyment of learning. (DfES, 2003: 4)

However, inspection evidence from Ofsted, the schools inspectorate, soon confirmed that reading in English schools was a specific area of concern as far as having fun went. A report significantly entitled *Reading for Purpose and Pleasure* (Ofsted, 2004), to which the PISA and PIRLS studies provided background, commented:

Although some schools were successfully raising reading attainment and were teaching pupils the skills they needed to read with accuracy and understanding, few were successfully engaging the interest of those who, though competent readers, did not read for pleasure. Schools seldom built on pupils' own reading interests and the range of reading material they read outside school. (p. 4)

Another report, *English 2000–05: A Review of Inspection Evidence* (Ofsted, 2005) described confusion and uncertainty amongst teachers as to how to teach reading and make it enjoyable within the constraints of the NLS:

Some teachers tell inspectors that teaching reading has lost its fun. It is certainly true that there is a good deal of uncertain practice, especially at Key Stages 2 and 3 [ages 7–11 and 11–14], as teachers try to develop shared and guided reading along-side previous practice. Is it appropriate or not any longer simply to read and share stories with their class; do they always need to analyse the text and set exercises? Is time for silent, independent reading regarded as good practice or not? Should teachers read whole novels with a class or is this a waste of valuable teaching time? In fact, Ofsted's evidence is that all these approaches, deployed appropriately, have potential, particularly as part of a systematic and balanced policy on reading.

Teachers often make use of texts without adequately considering their impact upon the pupils. They appear to regard texts primarily as a means of teaching writing: a poem is mined for its use of adjectives, metaphors and contrasting short and long sentences without attempting to engage pupils' personal response to the ideas and feelings it expresses. The text becomes a kind of manual rather than an opportunity for personal response to experience. This can then lead teachers to choose any text, irrespective of quality, instead of choosing the most appropriate texts for different purposes. (www.ofsted.gov.uk)

The report highlighted areas for improvement, including:

- making time to monitor and support pupils' wider, independent reading;
- improving links between Key Stages 2 and 3 in the reading curriculum and assessment;
- developing the role of school libraries and librarians in promoting independent reading;
- reviewing the approach to the whole class study of texts and authors to ensure that it contributes more powerfully to promoting positive attitudes towards reading.

(www.ofsted.gov.uk)

There next followed a startling public statement by the then Chief Inspector of Schools, David Bell, in a speech on World Book Day in 2005, when he frankly admitted:

For too many young people today, the pleasures of reading are not open to them; either because they do not read well enough or because they have already decided that reading is not for them. (www.ofsted.gov.uk)

A parliamentary inquiry, *Teaching Children to Read* in the same year also concluded: 'Whatever method is used in the early stages of teaching children to read, we are convinced that inspiring an enduring enjoyment of reading should be a key objective' (House of Commons Education and Skills Committee, 2005).

However, this official recognition that enjoyment of reading was important and that there was a problem with children's attitudes to reading fell short of admitting that the blame lay with the approach of the NLS and it successor, the Primary National Strategy (PNS). David Bell came close to this, writing in *Celebrating Reading Connects* magazine in December 2005 (www.literacytrust. org.uk/campaign/Celebrating_Reading_Connects), when he commented: 'There has been an unquestionable rise in the standards of children's literacy since the NLS was introduced in primary schools in 1998. However, we need to re-establish the link between reading and pleasure ...' (p. 23). In the same issue, though, Mike Lloyd-Jones, a regional adviser for the PNS, denied any tension between the approach to developing reading skills of the PNS and nurturing children's appetite for reading (p. 7).

Reading Connects, which was being celebrated in these articles, is an initiative funded by the DfES in the wake of the findings from PISA, PIRLS and Ofsted. Run by the National Literacy Trust, *Reading Connects* was launched in September 2004 with a remit of trying to build, through the Internet, a network of schools that promote reading. Through the *Reading Connects* website, schools are 'offered the tools they need to get started on developing a whole-school approach to reading for pleasure or build on existing good practice' (www.literacytrust.org.uk/readingconnects).

There may have been no official admission that the NLS and later PNS has been an important factor in children's declining enjoyment of reading, but the direction of recent revisions to the curriculum for English in primary schools suggests recognition of this. For example, the United Kingdom Qualifications and Curriculum Authority's (QCA) consultation exercise *English 21* resulted in the document *Taking English Forward: The Four Cs*, which included the clear statement: 'Children are entitled to: discover and rediscover the pleasure of reading through responding imaginatively to great books, stories and poems' (QCA, 2006: 8). The ominously titled *Raising Standards in Reading: Achieving Children's Targets* (DfES; 2005) referred to the PIRLS findings about English children's less positive views on reading and described schools that are effective in raising attainment in reading in these terms:

> Teachers place great emphasis not just on children acquiring specific reading skills but also on promoting engagement and pleasure in reading and they know what to do when a child does not seem motivated to read. (DfES, 2005: 4)

This was echoed in the 'renewed' *Primary Framework for Literacy and Mathematics* (DfES 2006a), where it was claimed: 'The revisions emphasise the importance of reading independently and reading for pleasure,' and which certainly included the following learning objective for children under 'Engaging with and Responding to Texts': 'read independently for purpose, pleasure and learning' (www.standards.dfes.gov.uk).

In 2007, the UK government announced plans for a National Year of Reading to run throughout 2008, 'involving the whole of society in a wide-ranging national campaign to encourage and promote more reading'. The then UK Education Secretary, Alan Johnson, pledged that this initiative would 'promote reading for pleasure in the family and beyond and help to build a nation of readers'. Launched at the same time as a document called *Every Parent Matters*, the initiative was aimed particularly at encouraging more parental involvement with children's reading. Also targeted were boys; Mr Johnson announced that 'to help get boys reading we will put a boys' bookshelf in every secondary school library in the country containing positive, modern, relevant role models for boys', and subsequently published a list of recommended authors (www.standards.dfes.gov.uk). In a separate initiative, a Booktrust scheme to keep pupils reading for pleasure during the transition to secondary school was announced, which involved every child starting Year 7 receiving a free book from a list of 12 titles.

Research Evidence

As well as the international and national surveys mentioned above, there is a growing body of research evidence which suggests the importance of motivational factors in the development of children's reading. A recent report to the Scottish Executive Education Department, *Literature Circles, Gender and Reading for Enjoyment* (Allan et al., 2005: 5), sums up well the benefits of reading for pleasure:

> Children who say that they enjoy reading and who read for pleasure in their own time do better at school. Reading for enjoyment is positively associated with reading attainment and with writing ability (OECD 2002). Pupils who read for pleasure also demonstrate a wider general knowledge (Wells 1986), a better understanding of other cultures (Meek 1991), and more complex insights regarding human nature, motivations and decision-making (Cunningham and Stanovich 1998, Bruner 1996).

The significant link between reading motivation and reading attainment or progress is a particularly compelling argument for the importance of reading for enjoyment, and has been made by other researchers (Baker and Wigfield, 1999; Twist et al., 2004).

In the United States a strong case has been made recently for the value of what is called 'free voluntary reading' (FVR) to be part of the school curriculum. This is not new, of course. Recreational reading programmes were promoted in the 1970s and 1980s in the United States and it was then that approaches such as Sustained Silent Reading (SSR) were introduced. Advocates at the time argued that:

X The development of a love of reading is too important to be left to chance. A recreational reading program should be a conscious, planned part of every classroom program ... It promotes positive attitudes toward reading, expands experiential background, enhances automaticity and fluency, provides opportunity for practice in the use of context cues, and expands meaning vocabularies. (Spiegel, 1981: 4)

Today similar arguments are being put forward in the face of a strong movement in the United States towards more restrictive and prescriptive forms of reading instruction based on strict 'phonics first and only' approaches, which have led to a decline in the use of authentic literature in the classroom and an emphasis on reading 'fluency', as measured by the stopwatch, rather than reading for meaning. Stephen Krashen (2004), a passionate advocate of FVR, defines it in this way:

FVR means reading because you want to. For school age children, FVR means no book report, no questions at the end of the chapter, and no looking up every vocabulary word. FVR means putting down a book you don't like and choosing another one instead. (p. x)

Access to books suitable for FVR in school and outside is vital, since children who develop the reading habit are the more likely to achieve acceptable levels of literacy than those who do not. As Krashen points out, a fraction of the funding spent on testing and technology would provide access to motivating reading materials for all children (p. 76). It is ironic, as Krashen concludes, that: 'While it may not be true that everything that is good for you is pleasant, the most effective way of building literacy happens to be the most pleasant' (pp. 151–152).

Another recent US study, *Reading Matters: What Research Reveals About Reading, Libraries and Community*, presents compelling research evidence that pleasure in the reading experience itself is a vital motivational factor for readers and that: 'Readers who become proficient are those who enjoy reading and who do it by choice as a voluntary activity in their leisure time'. (Ross et al., 2006: 4, 45) Reading done in children's own free time emerges as an important factor: 'Research also shows that the amount of reading done out of school is consistently related to gains in reading achievement' (p. 46). Perhaps it is because reading for pleasure *is* pleasurable rather than difficult or hard work that there is reluctance to accept it as an essential ingredient in reading development rather than just the icing on the cake, or possibly the decoration on the top.

Research done, again in the United States, in the late 1990s on the key features of classroom practice associated with motivation to read presents some recurring factors. For example, Linda Gambrell, a researcher of long standing in this area, suggests the following:

- a teacher who is a reading model;
- access to a book-rich classroom environment;
- being able to choose books oneself;
- being familiar with books;
- social interactions with others about books;
- incentives that reflect the value of reading.
  (Gambrell, 1996: 20)

Julianne Turner puts forward a similar list of features of literacy activities that foster motivation:

- specific meaningful contexts, holistic activities;
- autonomy: motivating activities promote learner choice and control;
- social collaboration: peer teaching and learning;
- emphasising metacognition;
- setting high expectations;
- open tasks.
  (Turner, 1997: 183)

John Guthrie and others in their summary of classroom contexts that enhance literacy engagement also suggest the importance of activities that are:

- self-directing, featuring student autonomy in choice of topic, books, peers;
- metacognitive, containing explicit teaching of reading strategies, problem solving, composing;
- collaborative: involving social construction of meaning.
  (Guthrie et al., 1996: 323)

The elements of successful classroom practice which keep appearing in these and other research findings are the need for activities that are open and authentic, that take place in a reading environment where there is easy access to plenty of suitable texts and to an enthusiastic reading teacher, that feature pupil choice, collaborative learning and an approach where pupils are aware of what they are doing and how and why they are doing it. More recently *Reading for Change: Results from PISA 2000* recommends these same approaches for promoting positive attitudes to reading, but adds one further factor. As well as 'interesting texts, autonomy and collaboration (with peers)', the report adds 'real world interaction' (OECD, 2002), the importance of making links between reading inside and outside the classroom, showing how readers in the world beyond the school also read for pleasure as well as for a variety of other purposes in their daily lives. We will see many of these key factors demonstrated in the case study schools discussed in the chapters that follow.

Action Point

Imagine you are trying to convince a sceptical audience of the value of reading for enjoyment in the primary school. Review the background information and research evidence presented in this chapter. Pick out what you feel are the five points that present the strongest argument in favour of developing reading for pleasure in the primary school. List these as bullet points in what you feel is their order of importance.

Chapter 2

Becoming a 'Reading for Pleasure School'

Summary

Chapter 2 explores what is involved in becoming a 'reading for pleasure school' and provides an example of a Reading for Pleasure Action Plan which one school used. Factors discussed include: the reading environment, opportunities for independent reading and reading aloud in the school timetable, book clubs and special events, reading incentive schemes, the school library, links with parents and the local community, and school transition.

There is no single way to develop the reading culture of a whole school. However, what schools do need, before they begin, is an agreement amongst all the staff and the wider school community that reading, and reading for pleasure in particular, is a priority for development. Sometimes this can be formally recognised by inclusion in the School Improvement Plan or Literacy Action Plan, and sometimes the agreement can be part of a more informal initiative. The key factor is that not only are the headteacher and the senior management team fully behind the initiative, which is vital, but all staff are involved in discussing and planning the development. This means time needs to be regularly dedicated in staff meetings and training days to how the school should become a 'reading for pleasure school'. By its very nature, promoting reading for pleasure in the primary school, whatever form it takes to begin with, needs to have everyone on board: it will not work simply as a directive from above by school management. Instant transformation cannot be expected either: staffs need time to change the culture themselves and not see it as being imposed on them.

To get everyone on board, some of the research findings mentioned in the previous chapter can provide powerful arguments. Models of good practice can also be persuasive. These can be provided either within the school by subject leaders and by visitors such as local authority (LA) advisers and leading literacy teachers, or by visits to centres of excellence in other schools. As one subject leader I interviewed put it: 'It's getting people in, sending staff out, and allowing them the time to get the message for themselves rather than being told what to do. It's about slowly eating away at policies and procedures that make up the culture you want to change'. In one school, for example, teachers were invited to bring a children's book to each meeting to share with colleagues as a small way of gradually raising the profile and awareness of children's literature amongst the staff. Some schools and LAs also offer after-school reading groups which meet each month to give teachers the opportunity to read children's literature for pleasure and to share reactions to what they read.

The starting point for most schools, though, is usually a stock-taking exercise to discover where they are in terms of promoting reading. The *Reading Connects* network, for example, recommends starting with an audit of whole school reading which it has devised and which is available from its website (www.literacytrust.org.uk/readingconnects). This stock-taking should involve finding out what the children's views on the subject are, as well as the teachers' and the parents', through discussions or written questionnaires.

Lessons from the children

The children, as the most important partners in the enterprise, need to be consulted and to be firmly on board before any reading for pleasure venture sets sail. The children who contributed words and pictures to my Reading Surveys reflected a range of attitudes to reading, as expected, from very positive through lukewarm to very negative. For example:

- *I like reading because I'm lost in my own world.*
- *Reading is fun. Just because you READ, you can still be COOL!*
- *Reading is sometimes fun and most of the time boring.*
- *I think books are OK, but I won't spend a lot of my time reading. BOOKS SORT OF RULE.*
- *Reading is boring, it's for NERDS.*
- *Reading is the last thing I would want to do. I would rather die than read.*

The pictures the children drew to accompany both their positive and negative comments were a reminder that reading takes place in a social context for young people and is often bound up with considerations of identity and self-presentation, as in Figures 2.1 and 2.2.

An initial audit should also involve investigating the general reading environment in the school, the resources for reading in classrooms and in the school library, school policies and practices in English and across the curriculum, and extra-curricular activities and external links that promote reading for enjoyment. Once the school has identified where it is, the process can then begin of deciding how to get to where it wants to be and how to monitor progress towards this, as with the school described on page 18.

Figure 2.1   *Children's drawings about reading reveal the importance of self-image*

Figure 2.2   *Children's drawings about reading reveal the importance of self-image*

Case Study School

The Reading for Pleasure Action Plan set out in Table 2.1 was part of the wider Literacy Action Plan in this primary school. However, the newly-installed English subject leader drew up a separate action plan for reading for pleasure because 'I really wanted to push the love of reading, and children enjoying books and getting pleasure from them, as we did when we were children'. The benefit of actually having a plan was that it kept her on task for what she wanted to do. She began by carrying out a reading audit of all children and staff, and found out which books they liked and wanted to have in school. She tried to order books to reflect these findings, spending over £2500 in two years to provide better quality books for the classroom and library that reflected the children's interest and ability levels.

In addition to the developments listed in the Reading for Pleasure Action Plan, as part of the wider Literacy Action Plan the subject leader made ICT a big focus, with an emphasis on film literacy to inspire children in reading and writing, and more electronic Big Books for the interactive whiteboard. She also developed guided reading in the school by observing all teachers, giving them feedback and training, and identifying good models for them to follow. The assessment and tracking of children's reading progress was also reviewed.

The success criteria for the Reading for Pleasure Action Plan recognised that 'not all that counts is countable', so improvements in SATs (Standard Assessment Tests) results were not the only measure used. Children's evaluations of activities such as Book Week, for example, were important. But there was also a recognition, in the subject leader's words, that 'you can do things for the sheer pleasure of doing them'. She cited another kind of success criterion: a 6-year-old boy with emotional problems who worked with a volunteer adult reader and was a non-reader at the start of the Action Plan year but was an independent reader by the end of it. She remembered, 'During Book Week he came with his own money and bought *Green Eggs and Ham* by Dr Seuss. He then brought it to school every day for about the next three weeks and read it to everyone!' This was the sort of outcome that showed the real impact of a reading for pleasure initiative.

As the Action Plan in Table 2.1 recognises, there are four partners who need to be engaged in improving any aspect of a school:

- the staff;
- the children;
- the parents;
- the wider local community.

In the rest of this chapter, I would like to look at how all these partners can be involved in developing a 'reading for pleasure school'.

The Reading Environment

'It's lots of little things, not one big thing.' This was one subject leader's analysis of how reading for pleasure was promoted in her school. The 'lots of little

Table 2.1 *Reading for Pleasure Action Plan. Aim: to promote reading for pleasure across the school*

Target	Action Needed	Time Scale	Resources	Success Criteria	Achieved (Date)
To provide a range of opportunities for children to read for pleasure	Lunch time reading clubs Boxes of books for children to share on quiet playground Paired reading with another class Children to take library books home	From Autumn term 2	Teachers' time running clubs Boxes of books Timetabled paired reading	Children across the school participating in reading activities offered	
To raise parental awareness of reading clubs and websites. To increase parents' confidence and skill when reading with their children	'Help your child to read' leaflet for KS1 (distributed at Parents' Evening) 'Book Trusted' flyer distributed Puffin reading club Parents to help out at school listening to one-to-one readers	By November 2005	Leaflets copied 'Book Trusted' flyer copied Teachers' time on Puffin club Parents' time	Leaflets and club info distributed and parental interest, knowledge and confidence increased	
To give children the opportunity to express themselves through drama, linked to reading	Lunchtime drama club for Y2	From Autumn term 1	Lunchtime club	Children develop confidence in speaking and using texts to support drama	

Table 2.1   (Continued)

Target	Action Needed	Time Scale	Resources	Success Criteria	Achieved (Date)
To encourage reluctant boys to read	Kick into Reading project Male authors invited into school Wider range of suitable texts Use of film and drama in Literacy lessons (initially in Y2)	Spring term	Cost of new books Cost of film clips resource Time and cost of visiting authors (Investigate budget)	Boys reading for pleasure throughout the school	
To develop library skills	Teaching Assistants to take children to school library during Planning, Preparation and Assessment time to teach them library skills	Ongoing	Library	Children acquire basic library skills so that they can confidently visit a public library and find a book	
To develop links with the wider community	Local librarians to visit the school Kick into Reading project Local author visits Local hero visits to share own childhood reading experience Parents to listen to children read. Local trips	Ongoing throughout year	Time of librarians, authors, and local heroes Cost of involving the local community Parents' time	There are at least three events throughout the year where local people come into school to help motivate children to read	
To organise a whole school week-long event to promote reading	Book week	Spring term	Cost of visiting authors and local heroes Time organising and arranging events	A successful book week held that generates enthusiasm and interest in reading	

Acknowledgements are due to Wendy Long for permission to reproduce this Action Plan things' included reading aloud a lot and 'masses of book talk': sharing conversations about the books she and the children were reading, letting other children overhear these conversations, children recommending books to each other and to share with the class, books being passed around, shared and swapped. As another subject leader I interviewed put it, 'it's about catching children reading and thoroughly enjoying reading and then discussing those books they're enjoying', especially those brought from home, something the children are encouraged to do from the outset.

This is particularly important because some primary school children, particularly older ones, will not have the opportunity or inclination to talk about books at home. In my own research, I surveyed over 300 parents of pupils, whose reading attitudes I had previously investigated, from 22 different schools, and found that a third of the children did not discuss their reading at home, with the percentage being even higher for boys. With children of this age, my research suggested that talking about books at home was associated more with enjoyment of reading fiction even than being read to by parents: two-thirds of those who almost never talked about books at home did not enjoy fiction, whereas over 96% of those who discussed their reading at home every day did enjoy stories.

The personal interest and enthusiasm of the teacher manifested in many small ways every school day is clearly a key factor in creating a reading environment that promotes enjoyment in the primary school. Children need to see in their teacher a role model of a keen reader. As one of the teachers quoted above insisted, 'You have to enjoy reading yourself and show it! I've got to find enjoyment, and if I'm getting enjoyment, I can see the children are too'. The kiss of death for promoting reading enjoyment is the teacher who says, 'I'm not a great reader myself, but ...' Fortunately, most teachers do read for enjoyment out of school: a survey recently found that teachers were the group most likely to read for relaxation, 71% doing so compared with 56% of adults overall who read books for pleasure (Legg, 2006: 12).

It is important also to avoid giving a negative message about reading as part of the 'hidden curriculum' of the school. Using reading as a punishment, for example pupils having to stay in at break and read a book, is obviously not going to make reading an attractive option for children. More subtly, using reading as a 'holding' activity at transition points during the day devalues books: there is nothing more calculated to ruin the reading habit than forcing children to get a book out and stare at it for a few minutes whilst there is noise or movement going on which make absorption in the text impossible.

As well as the invisible ethos of the school, the reading environment also of course includes the very visible physical environment. In reading for pleasure schools, reading is celebrated publicly whenever and wherever possible. Teachers have their own favourite children's books on display in their classrooms and their current reading books are on their desks. The cover of the book each class is currently reading is displayed on the classroom door. Book and reading-related displays are not confined to classrooms, though there are plenty of them there, but can be found in prominent places around the school buildings and grounds: in the hall, corridors and entrance foyer, as well as outside on noticeboards in the school grounds, maybe featuring a 'poem of the week', or painted onto walls in the playground. Displays feature reading in all its forms, from print to electronic, and books from all cultures; they include children's work as well as teachers'; they are addressed to parents as well as children. Reading may also feature in the school logo designed by the children and present all around the school. Books, newspapers, magazines and comics are prominently displayed in classrooms throughout the school, as well as in the school library. Even the playground has a reading hut and story garden where children can take a box of reading materials at break times. The school's cyberspace is also a rich reading environment. The school webpage features children's book recommendations, celebrates authors of the month and has topical news on book matters; there are links to children's book websites and email correspondence with other schools about reading and writing. The school's telephone 'hold' tape features poems and book extracts read by pupils.

In addition to these many 'little things', there are plenty of 'big things' which primary schools as a whole school can do to stimulate interest in reading. Some of the big things mentioned below are new ideas, but others are certainly not new.

Action Point

Carry out an audit of the reading environment in a primary school or classroom, or in an early years setting. How many of the above features that promote reading for pleasure are present? What other positive features are present which are not described above?

Independent Reading

The provision of a regular time for independent, silent or quiet reading across the entire school during each school day used to be common practice in primary schools until the 1990s, and of course has continued in some schools. This time often used to go by acronyms such as ERIC (Everyone Reading in Class), DEAR (Drop Everything and Read), or USSR (Uninterrupted Sustained Silent Reading), always abbreviated in American schools to SSR, perhaps for political reasons! However, as Judith Elkin points out: 'Initiatives such as USSR and ERIC, which aim to promote and encourage reading by providing the opportunity to undertake reading during the school day, have often been casualties of the time-consuming effects of the NLS' (Elkin et al., 2003: 76).

This time works best when it is seen as a positive part of the reading curriculum rather than, as mentioned above, just a 'holding' strategy whilst the teacher is doing things such as taking the register or other administrative tasks. It works better when children can choose freely what to read, including non-fiction, comics or magazines, when they are genuinely reading for enjoyment and there is no automatic requirement to write about what has been read. This does not mean, though, that personal reading choices should not be developed and readers challenged by interaction with the teacher (Millard, 1997: 171). This can be a good time to model book choice to children by discussing clues offered by covers, blurb, author information, title and genre. Lower ability, inexperienced and reluctant readers will need most guidance in choosing books. Sometimes children simply look for the biggest book or the one with the most impressive cover. One teacher I interviewed cited the case of the less able reader who picked up a dictionary for 'free' reading because it was the thickest book available.

Independent reading works best when the teacher reads for pleasure too, as far as that is possible. This model of adult reading can be very effective, as one teacher commented: 'They'll just suddenly look up and see that you're reading, you're concentrating and then they don't talk, they just get on with it'. Independent reading works best of all when everyone in the school reads during this time, including non-teaching staff, though in today's busy primary schools this is harder to achieve. If time is really pressing, independent reading for pleasure can be used as a 10-minute starter activity before literacy lessons, with the teacher also reading for enjoyment.

Case Study School

In this classroom, 'quiet reading' takes place twice a day, first thing in the morning and after lunch. During the course of a year, the Year 6 children become more used to coming in and picking up a book. Every classroom in the school has its own specific quiet reading time. The Y6 teacher feels it is a skill children need to learn: sitting still with a book for 15–20 minutes. She reads herself at the same time, and tries to model reading for pleasure. However, she feels that some teachers in the school still think it's a bit of a 'cheat' to sit there reading a book.

Stephen Krashen in *The Power of Reading: Insights from the Research*, confirms that the research evidence is clear that 'children read more when they see other people reading', as when the teacher reads in this way during silent reading, and that this kind of direct encouragement to read works most effectively when reading material is appropriate, self-selected and interesting. Pupil choice is particularly important (Krashen, 2004: 85). The international PIRLS survey of 10-year-olds found evidence of a clear link between independent reading and reading attainment: 'In England, as in the majority of countries, there was a positive association between the frequency of opportunities to read independently (defined as when pupils read silently, on their own, books of their own choosing) and reading achievement' (Twist et al., 2003: 65).

Case Study School

This Year 2 teacher has a 'silent reading' time most days. She builds up the infant children's independent reading stamina gradually over the year from 10 minutes by five-minute intervals up to 30 minutes. She feels this is still an important part of daily routine, to have to sit down and read each day. She comments, 'Personally I think that has brought most of my children on in terms of their independent reading. Children almost surprise themselves; they're so pleased when they find they can read books'.

Some teachers who use independent reading regularly report the need to vary the format to provide more focus and rigour in the sessions. This can mean, for example, extending independent reading to include the teacher working with individuals or small groups of children, rotating boxes of books relating to specific genres around the children, having paired reading, giving children access to audio books and books on computers, and having a plenary session at the end to discuss the reading done (Barrs and Pidgeon, 1993: 122–123). Other teachers working within the requirements of the NLS *Framework* report that they combine independent reading with listening to individuals read aloud to them and with guided reading, when pupils read in ability groups, or they rotate these different reading activities during the week or between weeks.

Lessons from the children

A recurring complaint in both the quantitative and qualitative data from my research was that children themselves did not enjoy reading aloud in class, as compared to reading silently, and that this ordeal affected their enjoyment of reading. Forty-five per cent of the sample children rated themselves as poor or OK readers when they read out loud, compared with only 25% when asked about reading generally. The children particularly disliked reading aloud at school, where they felt other pupils might make fun of them, as opposed to reading to family members at home. The number of different comments here reflects the frequency with which this type of complaint was made within the sample:

- *When I read out loud it makes me think I'm not very good but when I read in my head I think I'm reading well.*
- *I think it is much easier to read in your head because it makes you concentrate more.*
- *I sometimes have the words clogged up in my mouth.*
- *I get a bit nervous when I have to read out aloud because sometimes the words don't come out right or I keep losing my place, but when I am reading to myself most of the time I am fine*

- *I feel scared of reading in front of lots of people because I think people will laugh at me and get bored.*
- *I like reading on my own because no one can say 'speak louder so I can hear you'. I like reading to my brother so he won't go and say 'talk louder'.*
- *I prefer to read to myself because I can read it at my own pace.*
- *I most like reading to myself so there's no stopping and interrupting.*
- *When I read in guided reading in class, when it's my turn to read I shake and feel that other people might think that my reading is not very good.*
- *I am OK reading to my mum. I feel not very comfortable reading for a teacher or member of staff. I feel silly when I read to a member of staff or a teacher.*

Reading Aloud

The teacher reading a book aloud to pupils must be one of the oldest features of the primary school curriculum, but, like independent reading, it has succumbed to time pressures in many schools. Certainly for Key Stage 2 (KS2) children in England (ages 7–11) the demands of the NLS and the NC meant that it ceased to be a regular occurrence for many or was replaced by the 'Shared Reading' which took place within the Literacy Hour. 'Story went out of KS2 for many years', commented one English subject leader whose school was one of those that retained story reading every day throughout the school as 'an opportunity for fun and enjoyment and to introduce a variety of genres and authors'. Even for younger children, story time, traditionally at the end of the day, was by no means sacrosanct. For those schools wanting to promote reading for pleasure, though, this is a 'big thing', a vital part of a whole school approach.

Case Study School

For one school, story time has its own invariable slot: the 3 o'clock spot. At this time, everything else stops and each class listens to the teacher reading aloud, most probably a story, but also non-fiction or poetry. As the school's subject leader says, 'I'm a big advocate of teachers taking time to read texts to children. I know some people consider it slightly old fashioned, but actually I think it's another way of hooking children into reading for pleasure'. She actively recommends books to other staff to use at this time each day.

In another school, story time used to be at end of day, but was often missed out because of time pressure. Now it has been moved to earlier in the day, so that a 15–20-minute story time follows immediately from independent reading each day. The emphasis is firmly on enjoyment and letting the power of the story or other text come through to the children without interruption. As another infant school teacher put it: 'The children have a story every day.

We always ensure we don't unpick the story as we're reading it the first time through so the children actually get the full sense of the story.' The children can choose the story for the day themselves from a 'reading for pleasure shelf' in the classroom. Every teacher has felt that thrill when the spell of story reading and story telling works its magic on even the most reluctant of listeners.

It is particularly important that older primary children encounter books read aloud at school, whether fiction, poetry or non-fiction. My research involving parents of Year 6 children found that by this age nearly half of children no longer heard books read aloud or read aloud themselves at home. A popular reading target for some schools recently has been '5-a-day': encouraging children to be 'healthy' readers by fitting in five bits of reading a day either as listeners or as readers. The majority of these five 'portions' of reading may need to be provided by books read aloud to them at school for many children. There are certainly schools which manage to provide this healthy reading diet, through literacy lessons, group reading, class novels and story times as well as independent reading. For these schools, this is also a chance to demonstrate to children that there is nothing wrong with having two or three books on the go at once. One infant school, though, which followed this regime, reported being criticised by the schools inspectorate, Ofsted, for spending too much time reading aloud to children: an unusual charge!

The challenge for the teacher using independent reading and reading aloud to develop children's reading for pleasure is how to embed these practices in the curriculum, so that they are not separate, add-on activities and as such prone to being cut to make way for an expanding curriculum. As Ivey and Broaddus (2001: 367) point out: 'More research is needed to examine the place and purpose of independent reading and teacher read-alouds and their connections to instructional and curriculum goals'. However, teachers in schools where these practices continue to flourish have often been able successfully to link story time to curriculum content: for example, reading aloud Michelle Magorian's *Goodnight Mr Tom* to accompany a history topic on World War Two, or Jacqueline Wilson's *The Suitcase Kid* to link with work in PHSE. Related titles on the same topic or by the same author are then made available for children to choose for independent reading time. Children's right to choose what they read at this time is still paramount, though, as is the teacher's need to choose a read-aloud text that is worth listening to in its own right, whatever its connection to curriculum content areas.

Reading Assemblies

Special assemblies dedicated to reading-related activities raise the profile of reading within a school and confer status on readers, such is the power of whole-school occasions run by senior figures in the school. Reading assemblies can feature outside speakers from the local community, or from wider afield, who have a story to tell about reading as part of their lives. Equally, teachers can take it in turns to present reading assemblies. In one school, two teachers read short cliff-hanger extracts from books of their choice and talked about why they chose their books, what made the books special for them, or about the authors. They ended by telling the children where to find the books in school, the local library or a bookshop.

Children can also regularly present reading assemblies. In one assembly Year 6 pupils presented a survey of all materials read in school during a week, not just books but also comics and Internet sites. As part of their ICT work, the children presented their results in bar graphs and reported their overall findings using a PowerPoint presentation. The results of their survey then influenced book ordering in the school. Individual children can also give presentations to smaller year group assemblies about why they enjoy reading and what they like to read.

Book Clubs

Just as adult reading groups have flourished in recent years (and many school staff have set up their own), so school book clubs have become an increasingly popular part of the extra-curricular life of primary schools. These usually happen at lunchtime, though sometimes after school. They follow different patterns. For example, one school runs a School Story Club where the headteacher reads aloud a 15-minute story for any Year 3 and Year 4 children who want to attend. The children themselves request books they would like to hear. In other schools, the clubs run more along the lines of adult book groups: all children read the same book or part of a book each week and come along to talk about it, share favourite bits and read some more. Other clubs feature different books by particular authors each week. Sometimes the book club consists of children sharing book recommendations with the group, based on what they have been reading over the past week, and taking part in activities such as making bookmarks or bookplates. Book clubs can also be based on particular interests of groups of pupils, such as fantasy fiction series or comic books, and can be linked to music and cinema, such as a 'Book of the Film' club.

Case Study School

This after-school book club is run jointly by the school's English subject leader and a local librarian. Between eight and 20 children attend each week from across the school age-range, from Year 2 to Year 6. Children chose the name of the club and have designed the membership forms, logo and publicity materials. The club is currently focusing on the Kate Greenaway prize shortlist of picture books and is shadowing the judging by posting its comments on the prize's website (see Book Awards below).

A challenge for any school book club is to get enough boys to come along. Some schools tackle this by having Boys' Own Book Clubs, where boys get to choose which books to read, how they want to talk about them and when and where they want to meet. A Girls' Own Book Club can be run along the same lines, of course. One school provides the boys' reading club with its own room where they can store books, comics and magazines and put up posters and displays. Fathers and grandfathers are also invited in to talk about their favourite boyhood reads or just to read along with their sons and grandsons. A book such as *The Dangerous Book for Boys* by Hal and Conn Iggulden (2006), for example, provides an interesting non-fiction text for these different generations of readers to read and talk over together. There is no shortage of fiction material either: publishers have shown a lot of interest in recent years in bringing out, or sometimes reissuing, deliberately 'retro' styled books for boys and men, usually traditional adventure stories. Other schools have a dedicated 'school reading room', separate from the library, where any children and parents can choose to read out of lesson time.

Breakfast clubs are becoming increasingly common as primary schools are encouraged to expand the hours they stay open each day. Reading the back of a cereal packet was often said to be some children's main reading experience of the day, and some schools have built on this inclination to browse print over breakfast by introducing reading opportunities into breakfast clubs, making newspapers, magazines, comics and books available to children at this time. One school invites dads in also to read the morning newspapers with boys over breakfast, with positive results for the boys' motivation to engage with print.

Schools that are not able to provide their own book clubs can encourage children to join ones organised by local libraries. The Chatterbooks project run by The Reading Agency is a national scheme for 4–12-year-olds which encourages children and their families to join reading groups in public libraries. Members receive reading lists, review notes, reading diaries and games, and author tours are organised which can be shared with local schools As well as encouraging children to be more adventurous in their reading and giving them the opportunity to share their enthusiasm for books with others, organised reading groups like Chatterbooks also report significant improvements in children's speaking and listening skills as they gain the confidence to formulate and express their own views about their reading (www.readingagency.org.uk).

Book Awards

Many schools try to take part in the judging of children's book awards. Teachers report that involvement in national book awards creates a 'buzz' about books, makes reading matter and engages children's in-built interest in competitions of any kind, as well as raising the quantity and quality of discussion about books.

The most popular British book prizes to shadow are the Carnegie and the Kate Greenaway Medals, awarded in June each year, both run by the Chartered

Institute of Library and Information Professionals (CILIP) and judged by children's librarians. The award website gives the criteria used by the judges: 'The book that wins the Carnegie Medal should be a book of outstanding literary quality. The whole work should provide pleasure, not merely from the surface enjoyment of a good read, but also the deeper subconscious satisfaction of having gone through a vicarious, but at the time of reading, a *real* experience that is retained afterwards.' Since many books on the Carnegie shortlist tend to be novels for teenagers, most primary schools choose to follow the Kate Greenaway Medal, which features picture books: 'The book that wins the Kate Greenaway Medal should be a book of outstanding artistic quality. The whole work should provide pleasure from a stimulating and satisfying visual experience' (www. carnegiegreenaway.org.uk). There is a separate linked website for schools that want to register to shadow the two awards, where children can hear the shortlisted authors talk about their books, read the judges' weblogs, post and read book reviews, view voting charts, engage in debate about the books and of course cast their own votes, using the same criteria as the adult judges (www.carnegiegreenaway.org.uk/shadowings). Teachers and librarians also have their own pages on this site where they can get full information about the shadowing process. Of course, these two awards can be followed in schools anyway, without belonging to the official scheme, and many schools prefer to run their own judging.

Case Study School

This primary school has made the Kate Greenaway shadowing much more high profile this year, so every class is involved in the voting process. There is a shortlisted book of the day and Year 6 have responsibility for taking each of the eight books to other classes. After eight sessions, with one book shared each time, there is a voting day with a proper election process: two votes, one for a personal favourite and one for a class favourite. The children will then be able to compare their voting with how the books actually do in the real awards. Pupils are enthusiastic and say they enjoy the whole process of shadowing in this way.

The Nestlé (formerly Smarties) Children's Book Prize, run by the independent charity Booktrust, is organised so as to involve primary school children even more, since they are ultimately the judges. All children aged up to 11 can take part in the first round of judging; 50 classes from three age groups are then selected to become young judges of the prize in the second round, with the chance of attending the award ceremony in December. The aim is to involve as many young readers as possible in the process, as the website suggests: 'joining in with the Prize will help you introduce your class to some of the best new writing for children. The whole class can get involved in expressing their own ideas creatively and discussing their favourite books' (www.booktrusted.co.uk).

The Red House Children's Book Award is run by the Federation of Children's Book Groups (www.fcbg.org.uk), a charitable organisation that coordinates the many children's book groups run by parents, teachers, librarians and others throughout the United Kingdom. This award is promoted as the only major UK book prize decided by child readers alone, since children from the Federation of Children's Book Groups actually choose the shortlist of ten books before they are then voted on by any children who wish to take part, whether through school, home, book club or library. The children can vote for an overall winner as well as three category winners: Books for Younger Children, Books for Younger Readers and Books for Older Readers (see www. redhousechildrensbookaward.co.uk).

Schools can also take part in many regional awards for children's books run by local authorities. Also, there is nothing to prevent a school setting up its own book awards, along the lines of these major national prizes, and many do. The advantages here are obvious: the staff, parents and/or children can select the shortlisted books, organise the voting process, design an appropriate medal or trophy, and put on their own awards ceremony, with invited guests.

Book Days, Book Weeks and Book Festivals

Children's Book Week in UK primary schools in October and the international World Book Day in March have become established events in the primary school calendar and if the enthusiasm for books shown by many teachers and children on these occasions could be repeated every week, British children would certainly be world leaders in reading enjoyment.

Typically, Book Week involves authors visiting schools to give readings or performances and to run writing workshops, staff and children dressing up as characters from children's books, book fairs being run for parents and children, and a curriculum for the week which celebrates the joys of books and reading. Often schools use a theme for the week to provide a focus for the activities, such as Pirates, Space, or Books Round the World. Schools can get together with libraries, other primary schools, secondary schools and local bookshops to organise events. The Book Week website (www.booktrusted.co.uk) offers ideas and advice for schools planning activities.

Case Study School

During Book Week and World Book Day, one school organises cross-phase sharing of books. This is particularly successful because this multilingual school emphasises the importance of being an inclusive community in all respects. As the English subject leader says: 'It's just fantastic to be part of activities where for example Year 6 pupils work with Nursery children, reading and talking about picture books. It's amazing what children with English as an Additional Language (EAL) can get out of sessions like that'.

Book Week usually takes place in the first full week in October and so includes National Poetry Day, normally on the Thursday of that week. This is a chance to promote an often neglected area of children's literature, supported again by a website that offers guidance and suggestions for activities and events. For example, in one school all the children learn the same poem by heart during Book Week; in another school each class learns a different poem and all the classes come together to perform the poems on the Thursday. Each year there is a National Poetry Day theme which can be followed. Examples in recent years have been 'Food', 'The Future', 'Identity' and 'Dreams' (www.nationalpoetryday.org.uk).

Poetry in the abstract appears off-putting for many teachers, never mind pupils. Maybe memories of their own poetry lessons at school are still painful, particularly the feeling that poems studied had 'hidden meanings' which the teacher knew and you, the pupil, had to try to guess, usually unsuccessfully. Teachers who are still turned off by poetry have a chance to rediscover its pleasures for themselves by reading and sharing children's poems. There has never been a better time to do this, since the richness and variety of poetry written for children is greater than it has ever been. National Poetry Day is an excellent opportunity to turn negative experiences to good effect by making sure children today are not put off poems in the same way. Poems are for life, of course, not for a day, so National Poetry Day should be the start of reading poetry to children for enjoyment not a one-off activity.

Some schools make World Book Day in March the focus for another week of book-related celebrations and activities: book parties, quizzes, trails, fancy dress competitions, book sales, whole days given over to story-reading or storytelling of tales from different countries, even a 'sleep-over', where, for the morning session, nursery children bring in their pyjamas and bedtime book. One of the most attractive aspects of World Book Day is that it is a genuinely international event and so provides real opportunities for schools to get together with others around the globe to celebrate the role of books in many different cultures. Children can easily experience, via the Internet, how pupils enjoy reading in other countries.

Case Study School

During World Book Day, one school organised a School Book Swap. On this day each child brought in at least one book, if they could, maybe more, and each went home with a new book at the end of the day. The books to be swapped were all displayed in the hall, and Y6 children helped younger children to choose books suitable for them. Parents also had their own book swap, held under an awning in the playground at the start and end of the day. The English subject leader, who organised the event, commented: 'Parents were so pleased they asked if it could be done every month for adults. A definite hit and something any school could do: it involves no money!'

For many schools, World Book Day marks the start of a Readathon, lasting for three or four weeks, where children try to read as many books as they can in a given time and get sponsorship for doing this. In one school, each class 'adopts' a different author and the class tries to read as many books collectively as they can by 'their' writer. This can get round the problem of individual children reading widely different numbers of books during the Readathon, and so raising widely varying sums of money for charity, because of different levels of reading ability and stamina or parental support. All UK primary schools automatically receive World Book Day resource packs and £1 book tokens for all children in the school. The tokens can be spent on six specially published World Book Day books or in part-payment for any other books above a certain price. A website again provides support and ideas for events (www.worldbookday.com).

In addition to the book days and weeks that almost all primary schools celebrate, some schools hold their own book festivals at other times of the year. This means they can arrange visits by authors who are in heavy demand and therefore usually unavailable during national events. A school's own book festival, or a joint one held with a cluster of primary schools or with a local secondary school, also gives a strong message about how much the school individually values books and reading.

Case Study School

This school's book festival has become well known throughout the local area. It lasts for a week and includes visits by poets, storytellers and novelists to work with children throughout the school. The week's festivities culminate in a Literary Evening for parents at which children give presentations, read their work and introduce the star speaker, usually a popular children's author. The school's subject leader describes the festival as 'growing from small beginnings, like an acorn', beginning as a day event with a visiting author before extending to a whole week. The key to the success of this book festival is that both children and parents participate fully. A lot of preparation is done with children beforehand by all the teachers, and parents are involved during the week itself as well as attending the final evening. The festival helps develop parents' awareness of children's books and authors as well as the pupils'. For instance, the subject leader remembers parents initially being suspicious of Michael Rosen's poetry but after hearing him perform at the Literary Evening they were enthusiastic about sharing his poems with their children. She feels that the festival gives children the excitement of meeting authors – and that the effect lasts. The proof of this is that often pupils return from secondary school to attend the evenings and reminisce about writers they first encountered through previous book festivals.

Book Crossing

This is the name invented for the practice of 'releasing books into the wild' by leaving them in public places like cafes, buses and trains, or passing them on to someone else you know for them to read. The name and idea were the invention of Ron Hornbaker who created the www.bookcrossing.com website. This site allows the book releaser to register the book 'set free', give it a book crossing label and track its progress if other readers find it and write a journal entry on the website. The idea is rather like releasing a balloon with a message asking people to tell you when and where they find it. Though the book crossing website is a US one and not designed primarily for children, children's books make up the third largest category of books released and the site is suitable for children to use with supervision.

However, some schools have simply taken the book crossing idea and adapted it for their own school community. Initially, teachers leave the books in places around the school and grounds where individual children might find them, but the scheme can then expand so that children leave books of their choosing for others to find, although these have to be vetted by teachers first and the number in circulation needs to be regulated. Children can track where their books go, who reads them and what the readers think of them if a journal system similar to the website one is used.

Case Study School

In this school the scheme is called 'The Lost Reading Books'. Books are left around the school for children to find and read. The books are kept in plastic wallets and children write a sentence or two about the book when they have read it and leave the comments in the book for the next reader. Books can be taken home to read but have to be left somewhere in school for the next person to find. Finding a Lost Reading Book causes great excitement!

Incentive Schemes

There are many incentive schemes used by schools to increase reading motivation. Some of these are schemes devised by schools themselves, such as reading ladders or schemes that involve collecting badges or stars, where children can measure their progress and their achievements can be publicly recognised. One primary school, for example, has a regular 'Reader of the Week' award which is highly prized by pupils and can be awarded for a variety of achievements, including most improved reader, most helpful reading buddy, and so on. All the weekly winners are entered for a 'Reader of the Year' award, which is presented at the end of the school year at a special Awards Evening. Another school has its own 'currency' which children can earn through reading at home and then 'spend' on books from the school book fair: 'complete honest bribery, but it works', as one teacher described the scheme.

There are other incentive schemes which are external ones, such as the annual Summer Reading Challenge in the United Kingdom run by The Reading Agency in public libraries during the school holiday, which many schools actively publicise before the summer and follow up afterwards (www.readingagency.org.uk).

Children collect stickers on a card for each book borrowed and read up to a target of six titles. In 2007, for example, the summer reading promotion was called 'Big Wild Read' and used an environmental theme linked to a website www.bigwildread.co.uk, where children could play games, read blogs by writers, submit book reviews and share books read.

Schools also use commercial incentive schemes to promote reading. Accelerated Reader, produced by Renaissance Learning, is the most popular of these motivational reading programmes. Accelerated Reader works by getting children to complete computer-based quizzes involving comprehension questions after they have finished reading a school library book for which there is a quiz. A report is then automatically generated for the teacher on how well the child did in this quiz, and the teacher uses this feedback to help the child choose the next book to read. Many schools are enthusiastic about this programme and find that its computer quizzes are a powerful means of motivating children to read more. These endorsements and other evaluations can be read on the company's website (www.renaissance-learning.co.uk).

Other research, mostly from the United States, casts more doubt on the value of extrinsic reward schemes of this kind. Stephen Krashen concludes that research does not confirm the value of extrinsic reward schemes such as Accelerated Reader. He suggests that the greater access to books and the ability to self-select involved in Accelerated Reader may account for any gains, rather than points or prizes (Krashen, 2004: 122). In the United States there have been many other external reading incentive schemes which reward children for reading books with, for example, burgers, pizzas or, in the case of 'Bucks for Books', dollars. However, research does not show that these schemes increase intrinsic motivation in readers in the long term; when the rewards are withdrawn, reading engagement tends to return to its previous level. Those schemes that offered books as a reward for increased reading were more effective in the long run than those that offered non-book rewards. For instance, in the Running Start scheme, developed by Reading is Fundamental, children read to meet a specific goal, for example a certain number of books. They chose what they read and the incentive at the end was a book selected by the child. Studies revealed that participation in Running Start increased reading motivation in the long term. As the researchers observed: 'Incentives that reflect the value of the desired behaviour can be used to enhance intrinsic motivation' (Gambrell and Marinak 1997: 205). There was also a strong correlation between pupil choice and the development of intrinsic motivation. The same research suggested that teacher praise and feedback can actually be more effective than external incentives.

Pause for Thought

Have you ever given children incentives to reward reading? Did you ever receive incentives to read yourself as a child, either at home or at school? What were they and why were they introduced? Did they work? If so, for how long?

Reading Is Fundamental (RIF) is another initiative of the National Literacy Trust and was established in the UK in 1996, following its success in the United States. RIF works with children living in disadvantaged areas to promote reading for pleasure and encourage life-long reading as a way of addressing the cycle of educational underachievement. The scheme emphasises the principles of children choosing and owning books, as mentioned above, and also sharing them with their families at home. Schools as well as other organisations can apply for funding to run projects that have these aims. As the RIF website explains:

> Primary and secondary school-based RIF projects are run by teachers, school librarians or other staff members. They usually involve one or two entire year groups, or an alternative inclusive group such as a breakfast or after school club. Children usually choose one book a term over the course of the school year at events such as author visits, book character fancy dress days, trips to the library, storytelling sessions or book-related arts and crafts. Support with choosing books and hosting events is often provided by the public or schools library service and the project can provide excellent opportunities for parents to get involved. School projects can involve either a single school or a cluster of schools in the same local authority. (www.rif.org.uk)

Case Study School

This was how one primary school, which applied successfully to RIF for funding, described its experience of the scheme: 'They encourage you as a school to take part in reading awareness weeks or days, where you would focus on one book, maybe in KS1. You might make a bookmark, have posters and competitions, and they will send you money to either buy free books or give you money for an event, to bring in somebody like a storyteller. We took the children last year to the Roald Dahl story centre [in Great Missenden, Buckinghamshire], which is marvellous, and then we were sent a Roald Dahl book for each child to keep.' The school valued its involvement with RIF greatly and wholeheartedly recommended it to any other schools who felt they would qualify for funding.

School Libraries

The library needs to be the hub of any reading school, the centre to which all reading activities in the school lead. Sadly, this is not always the case and frequently the primary school library finds itself relegated to a corridor or a corner somewhere inaccessible, essentially a storage space rather than the heart of a reading community. Often also, the school library is purely a non-fiction collection. Sometimes it is completely supplanted by the computer room, giving children a very negative message about the value of books. Where there is a library, it may have to double as a sick room or a holding bay for those who misbehave. However, the school library does seem to be making a come-back: some of the schools I visited for my research had realised what they had lost when the library ceased to be at the centre of things and were making plans to reinvest in it and restore its position. One school was planning an unusual centrepiece for its new library: a bathtub, since that was the place the staff associated most with reading for pleasure!

The equation between good library provision and reading engagement is a simple one, as Stephen Krashen explains: 'When children have access to more books at home, at school, or at the public library, they read more'. He stresses the importance of a print-rich environment, since research shows that enriching classroom and school libraries results in more reading. Access is also an important factor: 'Students take more books out of school libraries that have more books and stay open longer'. Planned library visits also increase children's reading (Krashen, 2004: 58).

A recent report from the schools inspectorate Ofsted, *Good School Libraries: Making a Difference to Learning* (2006), identified those factors that help to produce good libraries in primary and secondary schools. It emphasised the importance of:

- the commitment and support of headteachers;
- the appointment of specialist library staff;
- effective monitoring and evaluation;
- coherent programmes for developing pupils' library skills.

Case Study School

This school illustrates all the factors listed by the inspectorate. The school management have made a funding decision to employ a part-time librarian and to allocate substantial funds for new books this year, emphasising the importance they place on the school library. As with any funding decisions, the outcomes are carefully monitored. The librarian is also involved with the local Schools Library Service and is well informed about new children's books. She ensures the school library is well stocked with new fiction and gives children an up-to-date list of authors to look out for. She also runs regular library skills lessons with Year 3 and Year 4 children. Each year the library has themed displays and decorations, for example the rainforest, to make it an attractive and exciting place for readers of all ages to visit. A thumbprint system is used for issuing books and children can borrow fiction and non-fiction freely to take home.

The vast majority of primary schools, of course, do not feel able to employ specialist library staff. Also, when budgets are tight, links to the local Schools Library Service (SLS) are sometimes the first to go in any cutbacks. This is particularly sad since the SLS, where it still exists, provides access to professional expertise in librarianship and children's literature, which may well not be available elsewhere in the school. In the absence of support from the SLS, schools often rely on parents and the children themselves, alongside the responsible member of staff, to run libraries and these dedicated volunteers can also make a real difference.

Case Study School

This school uses a large room for its extensive library, with workspaces where pupils can read and carry out tasks. There is no specialist librarian, but parents help with the library and assist pupils in choosing books. Children are also involved in running the library, issuing books and helping to order new stock. All children in the school have contributed to a 'wish list' of new books for the library by recommending books they have enjoyed. The English subject leader has had a major overhaul of book stock and books are now displayed more attractively, often front-on as in bookshops. She has also added story sacks to the loan collection. The room has been made into one that teachers want to go into and use, so that it is now also used for English lessons and for reading aloud sessions as well as for library skills lessons. Teachers give children a weekly task to do, which involves them using the library independently.

School libraries, like public ones, do have an image problem. Ross et al. (2006) report young people's views to the effect that: 'Libraries are not cool; they are frequented by nerds, dorks, and dweebs'. Young readers also complain that librarians are unapproachable and libraries too quiet (p.112)! My own research found that even in primary schools that were successful in promoting reading for pleasure, the majority of children were still negative about libraries. Only 47% of over 1400 children questioned thought libraries were a great or interesting place to spend time; for the other 53%, including 49% of girls, they were an only an OK or a boring place. A similar picture emerged when I surveyed the parents of these children. Nearly half of the sample of over 300 parents said their children almost never went to the library and only 4% said their children went weekly. These children were again keen readers; nearly three-quarters of those who almost never went to the library enjoyed reading fiction quite a lot or very much. Levels of book ownership had no effect on the frequency of library visits.

Lessons from the children

There were repeated complaints from children in the responses to my Reading Survey that school and classroom book stocks were not interesting or up-to-date. For example:

- *There aren't any good books for quiet reading.*
- *I would like to have more exciting books to read at school and to go in the library to get books and have a bigger range of books to choose from.*
- *I like to sometimes read comics or X-Men comics. The school has quite old books but I want them to have new ones.*

Those schools that have managed to overcome this negative perception of the school or classroom library have done so with a variety of imaginative ideas, in addition to regularly renewing book stocks. For example:

- introducing library 'loyalty cards' to reward regular borrowers;
- holding parents' events and activities in the school library;
- allowing parents to borrow books;
- having an author of the month featured in the library;
- expanding library stock to include newspapers, magazines and comics;
- arranging book 'blind dates', where children can take home books in plain wrappers to try out before deciding whether to read them in full;
- holding book 'speed dating' sessions, where children are introduced to different books and have a few minutes with each to decide which they want to take out. 'Speed dating' can also involve a group of readers spending a minute at a time recommending a book to each other; at the end of the session, each reader decides which book to 'take out';
- holding themed book events, such as a 'Murder in the Library' game, where pupils have to solve a mystery or a crime involving books; or a book Treasure Hunt, which involves searching for clues in books to find some hidden 'treasure'.

The extending of school hours presents great opportunities for expanding the role of the school library. In some schools that have extended opening, the library is open in the morning before school starts and again at the end of the day. This means, for example, that children who cannot do research at home or in a local library can also also use special areas set aside in the school library for homework. But the school library can also be open at other times during the day to involve parents and promote the library facilities, for example having tea and coffee afternoons for parents or lunchtime library clubs for children.

Case Study School

In this school, the library redevelopment came about because of a Reading Connects audit. The room was completely refurbished with new book stock and now has a librarian for half a day a week, who looks after all the administration. The school works closely with the local SLS, who audited the library stock and now provide the entire non-fiction collection. The school is also involved in a pilot project with the SLS, in partnership with a local secondary school, for developing an open library system as part of extending school hours. Every class in the school has a library slot and children can also go and change their books during lunchtime each day. Children are allowed to borrow anything they want. The library is also part of the school's incentive scheme: the house that wins most team points wins an extra library session at lunchtime.

Even when there is a thriving central library in the school, classroom libraries are still very important, especially for fiction. Where there is no whole school library, or no fiction in the library, then class libraries become vital. They provide children with close daily contact with reading materials and make a statement about the status of reading in the classroom. Anecdotal evidence suggests there is a decline in the provision of 'book corners' and where they are present the stock is often not up-to-date or invitingly displayed. In schools where reading for enjoyment is successfully promoted, well-maintained classroom collections are a key feature, involving a regular inflow of carefully chosen new reading material, replacement or discarding of old stock, displays to stimulate interest in books and authors, and active participation by the children in choosing new stock and running the class library.

Involving Parents

Involving parents is a vital part of any campaign to promote reading for pleasure in the primary school. International research studies, such as the PISA survey of 2000, have shown that parents who read to children, listen to them read, talk to them about reading and have reading materials available for them at home, are more likely to raise children who enjoy reading and therefore do well at school. Parental engagement in children's reading, as mentioned in Chapter 1, was a more important factor in children's attainment in reading than parental occupation (OECD, 2002).

Recent research reveals the importance of parents' listening to children read as well as reading to them, particularly for less able younger pupils (Bloom and Marley, 2007: 30). My own research suggests the importance of parents *talking* to older primary pupils about books. In my survey of parents, as mentioned above, discussion of reading within the home emerged as an even more important factor in children enjoying books than parents reading aloud to them. In an era of 'crossover' books, such as those of Philip Pullman and J.K. Rowling, sharing reading with older children can easily mean both adults and children reading the same book and swapping impressions. A recent study of 1226 adults, for instance, revealed that 35% of them had read all the *Harry Potter* books, including 50% of teachers within the survey population (Legg, 2006: 12).

Most parents are very keen to help their children to read from the earliest stages, but with some this well-intentioned interest can translate into forcing children to read when they do not want to, drilling them inappropriately in skills, or pushing them to read a harder or longer book than is currently appropriate. The best way parents can help the teacher, usually, is by encouraging pleasure reading at home, by reading together with their children and talking about books read, rather than through trying to teach reading. Schools usually seek to monitor and support this home reading in a number of ways, most commonly through reading logs of various kinds, which work best when they are interactive journals where a three-way conversation can develop between parent, child and teacher. Some schools issue bookmarks for use with home reading, which act as a reminder to parents about best practice in supporting children's reading. Others have developed incentive systems using stickers that acknowledge and reward reading done at home: children receive a sticker for a certain number of books or pages read and collect their stickers in a booklet to qualify for prizes. There have also been some instances of schools using stickers to indicate that sufficient home reading has *not* been done, at which point a red warning sticker appears in the home-school reading log! This seems counterproductive to developing reading enjoyment at home and building partnerships.

Schools frequently organise meetings for parents to encourage and support reading at home. These work best when they involve pupils as well in some way and when they include parents of all age groups.

Case Study School

A reading evening was organised for parents of children throughout the age range of this primary school. The English subject leader tried to give parents an insight into how to help their children read, both in terms of initial reading skills for the younger pupils and comprehension and response for the older ones, with an emphasis on encouraging parents to talk about books with their children. The school produced simple handouts and booklets for new parents about 'how to help your children to read', which were designed and also translated into Urdu by Year 6 pupils.

Some schools take this further and invite parents to workshops where they can take part in reading activities such as their children experience in school.

Case Study School

One school was concerned that parents were not encouraging children to actually enjoy the reading their children brought home from school. This tended to be done as a chore rather than a pleasure, or as the subject leader put it: 'The parents tend to just see it as them sitting down for ten minutes and reading, reading, reading, and then right that's it, finished, rather than enjoying the sitting-under-the-bedclothes or curling-up kind of reading which is how we want people to read really'. So she organised an English evening lasting a couple of hours. 'This was a very new thing for our school,' she reflected afterwards, 'but it was brilliant. It was basically to show the parents what we are doing, but also to show them how they can help at home and I think they were very surprised at the amount that the children had to do and the depth in which they had to do it.' The parents carried out the kind of response activities that their children would normally do with the text and discovered there was more to reading that just getting the words right. 'We used *Goodnight Mr Tom* as an example and the parents were struggling themselves!'

Other schools invite parents in to observe or take part in demonstration guided reading sessions, often during morning assembly time, where the emphasis is on active rather than passive reading, on modelling reading for meaning and for enjoyment. Some schools go even further than this and invite parents in to be involved with their child's reading during lesson time.

Case Study School

Parents' Mornings work extremely successfully in this primary school. Once a fortnight on a regular basis, parents come in and work alongside their child with whatever they are doing, including reading, for 30–40 minutes or longer as the children get older. This happens from the Reception class right through to the end of KS2. In addition, there are reading mornings at KS2 when parents are invited by letter to come in and read with their child for 20–25 minutes. These reading mornings happen every week in the library area, on a different morning for each class. The challenge, the school feels, is to keep parents interested when their child has become an independent reader; fewer parents tend to be involved by Year 6 however, having been very keen at the start, since they feel they don't need to do anything by then.

Schools also get parents on board for reading promotion in a variety of other ways, apart from those already mentioned. For example:

- inviting parents to author visits and other daytime book events;
- holding regular book fairs for parents;
- holding evening book quizzes and reading-related events;
- 'new books for old' events, where parents bring in books their children have outgrown, which are then sold to help purchase new ones;
- inviting parents to assemblies celebrating reading;
- getting pupils to do surveys of parents' childhood reading;
- asking parents in to talk about their reading experiences.

Recent UK government initiatives have also recognised the vitally important contribution parents make at home to children's development as readers. In announcing the National Year of Reading in 2008, the then Education Secretary addressed this contribution directly:

One of the most important things a parent can do to boost the educational chances of their children is to read to them. Simple yes – but in a busy world it doesn't happen enough. Thirty per cent of parents don't read regularly with their young children – a vital but missed opportunity to boost their children's development. We watch an average of four hours television a day. If we read to our children for just a tenth of this every day, we'd give their chances a massive boost. (www.dfes.gov.uk)

The Family Reading Campaign was launched at the beginning of 2007 to encourage reading at home and raise awareness of its importance in many areas of life, including schools (www.familyreading.org.uk). The *Reading Connects Family Engagement Toolkit*, produced as part of this wider campaign, was specifically aimed at supporting schools in their efforts to reach out to children's families. This contained practical ideas, case studies and resources such as editable activity cards, leaflets and posters, designed to help schools make homes into 'reading homes'. The campaign was planned to coincide with the launch of the parent strand of the BBC's RaW (Reading and Writing) campaign. The BBC produced a parents' storytelling pack – stories, stickers and ideas to help support parents in reading with their children (www.bbc.co.uk/raw/campaign).

Involving the Wider Community

Schools striving to promote reading for enjoyment need to give children opportunities for 'real world interaction', in the words of the PISA study (OECD, 2002). This is a way of opening the doors and windows of the reading curriculum, letting in some fresh air and blowing away some of the cobwebs.

Case Study School

A display board in a prominent position in one school became the focus for a whole-school effort to raise the profile of reading by showing children that 'reading happens all around them'. Each week the board featured members of staff as readers, not only teachers, but also kitchen staff, cleaners, the lollipop man and other adults who regularly worked in the school and the local community. The display included photographs of them reading, information about what they enjoyed as readers, book recommendations and so on. As the English subject leader commented: 'We wanted just to do something a bit extra to show that adults read as well. One of our objectives was to help everybody appreciate that reading helps them in one way or another, to actually value the fact that we can read. We wanted to raise everyone's awareness about what a great thing it is to be able to read'.

This idea of a 'Get Caught Reading' campaign featuring school staff originated with the Reading Connects network. Schools have extended it, for example, by including in their displays fun pictures of parents reading, by getting older children to take photos of younger ones reading, and by capturing moments of 'extreme reading', in other words people reading in unusual situations such as a crane driver or a window cleaner. Sometimes these photographs are part of a 'Guess Who?' competition, where the face of the adult or child is hidden by the book they are reading and their identity has to be guessed on the basis of what they are reading.

Other schools invite adults from the local community to take part in assemblies and literacy lessons where they talk about the part that reading plays in their lives. Local police officers, fire fighters, business people, sports coaches from the nearby leisure centre and others talk about how reading is vital in many aspects of their daily work, as well as in developing their careers through study. They also talk about the reading they do for pleasure, to help them relax during breaks and at the end of the working day, and share the books, magazines, newspapers or websites that they enjoy reading in their free time.

Case Study School

This primary school made links with the local professional football club to promote reading. Footballers came to the school and talked about how reading both fiction and non-fiction for enjoyment fitted into their lives, for example during long coach journeys to matches, in their leisure time after training sessions, and as a way of being able to switch off and deal with stress. They also showed how they used books, magazines and the Internet to help develop themselves as professionals, some working for coaching badges, others interested in biographies of well-known players and managers or personalities in other sports.

In many schools, adult volunteers from industry come in and listen to children read, usually those pupils who need extra help for whatever reason. This arrangement works best when the volunteers have some training and are able to discuss books of different text types which they and the children have read, as well as play reading-related games and bring in resource packs. When this becomes an enjoyable activity that children look forward to it can be very motivating for reluctant or struggling readers by providing adult role models of real readers. Often partnerships are forged which can go beyond the classroom context, so that groups of children might visit the volunteers' workplaces to see how reading fits into the world of work. The main agency for primary school reading volunteers in England is Volunteer Reading Help (www.vrh.org.uk or via www.timebank.org.uk). This organisation interviews all volunteers and provides the necessary Criminal Records Bureau (CRB) checks and training. In the Volunteer Reading Help scheme, the volunteer will typically work with three appropriate children identified by the teacher and will work with them twice a week, in two half-hour sessions, for a whole year, to ensure continuity.

Perhaps the most obvious link to make with the wider local community is with the school's nearest public library. Libraries today have a remit that includes developing and advising readers, including children, so a connection with a local primary school helps all concerned. The Reading Agency, a UK charity that 'inspires, challenges and supports' libraries, has produced a pack

Enjoying Reading! which is designed to help libraries and schools forge stronger relationships in order to increase children's reading for pleasure (www.reading agency.org.uk). Often public libraries also have trained children's librarians who can offer specialist advice and support. Links can be at this advisory level or better still can involve visits by the children's librarian to school and visits by children to the library itself during school hours. Drawing on the human resources as well as the book stocks of the local public library can have a significant effect on reading within the school.

Case Study School

This school organised a special project with Year 5 reluctant and less able readers. The children were not making expected progress in reading and had negative attitudes, so the English subject leader decided that something needed to be done. The children were taken to the local library on Friday afternoon for the last hour every week for a term and a half. The children's librarian asked them what books they liked and arranged for these often brand new books to be available to borrow on the next visit. Some parents came and joined their children in the library. The children responded very positively to this project and attitudes to reading for pleasure improved as a result.

School Transition

Having nurtured the reading for pleasure habit in children, feeder schools are understandably keen for it to continue in the schools that children move on to, whether that means moving from infant to junior school, first school to middle, or junior school to secondary. The new 'big school', whatever it is, should respect and value the reading experiences children bring with them, encourage them to continue to enjoy what they currently read for pleasure, but also offer new and challenging reading opportunities that build on their past successes. However, many of the English subject leaders I spoke to in the course of my research felt more needed to be done in this area in particular. Partly because personnel in schools changes all the time, links had to be constantly renewed from year to year otherwise they simply lapsed and information about, for example, class readers used at KS2 was not passed on to KS3 English teachers. But still, too often, children started at their new schools as 'blank slates' as far as reading was concerned, although the feeder schools that they left knew them to be highly individual, often extremely avid and well-informed readers.

Many primary schools *do* have links that involve, for example, teachers from sending and receiving schools exchanging classes for a day, or secondary school librarians visiting primary schools to carry out book-related activities and talk about the children's reading. There are plenty of opportunities here for the new teachers and librarians to get to know children's reading attitudes, experiences and preferences and to share with the children their own. Other schools deliberately make links through outside agencies such as local libraries or book events in the schools or local communities. Here teachers and children from feeder and 'eater' school can get together in activities where reading for enjoyment is celebrated. All schools have preliminary visits by pupils where they meet their new teachers and see their new schools, and this can be the opportunity to make links in terms of reading preferences. Elaine Millard (1997: 174–5) mentions an effective scheme in one secondary school where new pupils have a book waiting in the school library for them on their first day, ordered by the child on a preliminary visit the previous term.

The UK government's recognition of the problem of children losing the reading for pleasure habit in the transfer from primary to secondary education prompted the extension of a scheme for giving free books to children. The original Bookstart scheme provided free packs of books for babies at different stages between 6 months and 3 years old, and Booktime then gave a picture book to children of age 4 or 5 shortly after they started primary school (www.booktime.pearson.com). In 2007 the scheme, operated by Booktrust, was extended to all Year 7 children (11–12 years) at the start of secondary education. They received a free book from a list of 12 titles, which included poetry, fiction and non-fiction (www.bookedup.org.uk).

Case Study School: KS1/KS2 Transition

This junior school arranged a shared story day with its feeder infant school towards the end of the summer term. Year 2 children and parents joined the Year 3 teachers in the junior school. The children were paired off with adults and put in small groups. The junior teachers provided objects as stimuli for story writing and also read and told stories to the infants. The Y2 children came up with ideas for stories and the adults scribed for them, as necessary. The shared story day worked very well as a way of building literacy bridges between the two schools for teachers, children and parents.

Case Study School: KS2/KS3 Transition

One junior school's links with its local secondary school involved an English specialism day when Year 6 children went to the secondary school for a Roald Dahl theme day, which included practical and fun activities such as making cakes and creating pop-up books. The same children also completed a PNS 'transition unit' on Michael Morpurgo's novel *Kensuke's Kingdom* and took their files from this work to secondary school with them when they left.

Action Point

Review the suggestions in this chapter. Pick out the three things which you feel would be the first priorities for you in developing reading for pleasure in a primary school. How would you introduce these initiatives? How would you then monitor and evaluate their effectiveness? Draft them out in the form of an action plan, following the example shown in Table 2.1.

Chapter 3

Promoting Reading for Pleasure in the Early Years

Summary

Chapter 3 focuses on how reading for pleasure can be developed in the Early Years Foundation Stage (0–5 years) and at Key Stage 1 (5–7 years). It investigates the impact of recent changes to the teaching of early reading in English schools, and looks in particular at how systematic synthetic phonics teaching relates to nurturing a love of books and reading in very young children. Specific, practical ways of promoting reading for enjoyment are suggested, based on the elements of successful classroom practice identified by research. The chapter also explores how reading for pleasure can extend across the curriculum and across different media, and this is illustrated with an example of real classroom planning from a school which demonstrates good practice. The crucial importance of involving parents in promoting reading enjoyment with young children is also emphasised.

Readers are made not born, as Aidan Chambers once pointed out (Chambers, 1973: 16). However, the UK government's Bookstart and Booktime schemes, mentioned in the previous chapter, have been attempts to start making readers as soon as possible after birth by distributing free books to parents. All children entering schooling in England should now have at least this minimum early experience of books behind them, though obviously the use to which individual parents put their free books will vary enormously. The Early Years Foundation Stage (EYFS) in England, which covers children's learning, development and care from 0–5 years, has also attempted for the first time in official documents to see children as readers in the making from birth onwards. The EYFS is linked to the government's *Every Child Matters* project which seeks to support all children, whatever their background or circumstances, so that they can:

- be healthy;
- stay safe;
- *enjoy and achieve*; [my italics]

- make a positive contribution;
- achieve economic well-being.
  (www.everychildmatters.gov.uk)

In the non-statutory *Practice Guidance for the Early Years Foundation Stage* (DfES, 2007b), children's development as readers is mapped out in six stages from birth to 60 months within the 'Communication, Language and Literacy' area of learning. As well as setting out these 'development matters', the guidance suggests how early years professionals should 'look, listen and note' during this development, and what 'effective practice' and 'planning and resourcing' are needed at each stage.

Interestingly, the development of 'Linking Sounds and Letters' is mapped separately from that of 'Reading' in this document, though clearly all the areas of early learning are meant to be interconnected and not dealt with in isolation. 'Linking Sounds and Letters' is concerned with children's increasing awareness of sounds, particularly rhyme, rhythm and alliteration, culminating in the development of phonic knowledge to use in reading and writing. This is supported by activities that explore sounds and develop phonemic awareness. Practitioners are asked to make 'principled professional judgements as to when individual children are ready' to start a programme of systematic phonic work, though it is stated that for most children this will be by the age of 5. The 'Reading' strand, on the other hand, focuses on children's developing interest in stories, poems and information texts, their familiarity with books and enjoyment of an increasing range of them. This is supported by telling and reading stories and poems, discussing them, modelling the use of information texts, encouraging children to handle books and providing a print-rich environment.

The *Statutory Framework for the Early Years Foundation Stage* (DfES, 2007c) sets out the early learning goals that English children should attain by the age of 5, having followed this progression as early readers. For the 'Linking Sounds and Letters' strand, the goals are that children should:

- hear and say sounds in words in the order in which they occur;
- link sounds to letters, naming and sounding the letters of the alphabet;
- use their phonic knowledge to write simple regular words and make phonetically plausible attempts at more complex words.

For the 'Reading' strand, children should be able to:

- explore and experiment with sounds, words and texts;
- retell narratives in the correct sequence, drawing on language patterns of stories;
- read a range of familiar and common words and simple sentences independently;
- know that print carries meaning and, in English, is read from left to right and top to bottom;

- show an understanding of the elements of stories, such as main character, sequence of events and openings, and how information can be found in non-fiction texts to answer questions about who, why and how. (DfES, 2007c)

Action Point

Brainstorm ways in which positive experiences of books and other reading material can be integrated into some of the other areas of learning and development of the EYFS as well as 'Communication, Language and Literacy'. The other five areas are

- Personal, Social and Emotional Development
- Problem Solving, Reasoning and Numeracy
- Knowledge and Understanding of the World
- Physical Development
- Creative Development

The challenge for schools when children enter the nursery or reception class is to build on their varying experiences of the stages of early reading as detailed in the EYFS and to ensure children progress towards these learning goals. It is a crucial stage in establishing enthusiasm for books and reading; positive attitudes created here can set the pattern for life.

Case Study School

The teachers' and other adults' first priority when children enter the nursery class of this infant school is to enthuse them about books. The whole staff try to give the new entrants as positive an experience of books as possible right from the start, especially those not from bookish homes. A book-rich reading environment in the whole school and in individual classrooms is seen as vital, so in addition to appropriate environmental print, the nursery has changing book displays and book boxes, as well as a range of other reading materials. Books and reading are integrated into all areas of learning as far as possible, as the school lays the foundation for what it sees as not just lifelong reading for pleasure but lifelong learning for pleasure. The nursery is fully included with the rest of the school in all reading-related special activities such as Book Week.

The renewed *Primary Framework for Literacy and Mathematics* (DfES, 2006a), which is non-statutory but almost universally followed in English primary schools, sets out the core learning in literacy for children at Key Stage 1, as well as adding some additional Foundation Stage objectives to the Early Learning Goals. Like the EYFS, it has separate strands for different aspects of reading development: strand 5 'Word Recognition: decoding (reading) and encoding (spelling)' on the one hand, and strands 7 and 8 'Understanding and Interpreting Texts' and 'Engaging with and Responding to Texts' on the other.

The 'Word Recognition' strand gives the outline of a systematic phonics programme whilst the other two strands focus on reading comprehension, in terms of developing reading for meaning, exploring the structures of fiction and non-fiction texts, engaging with and responding to books, and expressing personal preferences in reading. Unfortunately, there is no mention of either 'enjoyment' or 'pleasure' in these three reading strands for Years 1 and 2 of the *Primary Framework*.

However, the National Curriculum (NC), which the *Primary Framework* is meant to deliver, *does* use those words when it summarises Reading at KS1 in the following way: 'pupils' interest and pleasure in reading is developed as they learn to read confidently and independently'. Also under 'Reading Strategies', the NC originally gave as its first objective: 'To read with fluency, accuracy, understanding and enjoyment, pupils should be taught to use a range of strategies to make sense of what they read' (www.nc.uk.net), though significantly this wording was altered from September 2007 to read: 'Pupils should be taught to read with fluency, accuracy, understanding and enjoyment', removing the reference to using 'a range of strategies' (Wyse and Styles, 2007). This is in spite of Ofsted's findings, as expressed by the then Chief Inspector of Schools, David Bell, in a speech for World Book Day on 2 March 2005, that: 'Our evidence confirms … that the most successful schools do indeed recognise the importance of introducing pupils to a broad range of strategies including the teaching of phonics' (www.ofsted.gov.uk).

Pause for Thought

Is it important to teach children 'a range of strategies' to make sense of print when they are beginning to learn to read? If so, what is the value of this? Or is a range of strategies confusing for both children and teachers? If so, what is the value of emphasising just one strategy, such as phonic decoding?

The Teaching of Early Reading

The amendment of the NC to delete reference to 'a range of strategies' followed the independent review of teaching of early reading in English primary schools by Jim Rose in 2006. This 'Rose Review' (DfES, 2006b) recommended that:

High quality systematic phonic work as defined by the review should be taught discretely. The knowledge, skills and understanding that constitute high quality phonic work should be taught as the prime approach in learning to decode (to read) and encode (to write/spell) print. Phonic work should be set within a broad and rich language curriculum that takes full account of developing the four interdependent strands of language: speaking, listening, reading and writing and enlarging children's stock of words. (p. 70)

The Rose Review defined 'high quality systematic phonic work' in this way: 'Despite uncertainties in research findings, the practice seen by the review shows that the systematic approach, which is generally understood as "synthetic phonics", offers the vast majority of young children the best and most direct route to becoming skilled readers and writers' (p. 4). The key features of a synthetic phonics approach are described in the Review (p. 20) as teaching beginner readers:

- grapheme/phoneme (letter/sound) correspondences (the alphabetic principle) in a clearly defined, incremental sequence;
- to apply the highly important skill of blending (synthesising) phonemes in order, all through a word to read it;
- to apply the skills of segmenting words into their constituent phonemes to spell;
- that blending and segmenting are reversible processes.

The Rose Review put forward a new model of reading, the Simple View of reading, to replace the previously recommended Searchlights model. The Simple View treats word recognition processes and language comprehension processes as 'separable dimensions of reading' in a way not proposed in the earlier model. Although it is made clear that both processes are essential at all phases of reading development, the emphasis is to be put on the establishment of fluent automatic word recognition skills in the early stages, since this is a 'time limited task' whereas language comprehension is lifelong (pp. 77–78).

Although its remit was to consider only phonic instruction as part of the teaching of early reading, the Rose Review acknowledges that this is far from being the whole of reading and that promoting enthusiasm for reading is also vital:

It is widely agreed that phonic work is an essential part, but not the whole picture, of what it takes to become a fluent reader and skilled writer, well capable of comprehending and composing text. Although this review focuses upon phonic work, it is very important to understand what the rest of the picture looks like and requires. For example, nurturing positive attitudes to literacy and the skills associated with them, across the curriculum, is crucially important ... (p. 16)

In 2007, *Letters and Sounds: Principles and Practice of High Quality Phonics* (DfES, 2007a) was sent to all primary schools in England, containing notes of guidance and a six-phase teaching programme, illustrated by an accompanying DVD. *Letters and Sounds* replaced previous government materials supporting phonics teaching. It was based on the principles set out in the Rose Review and aligned with the objectives in the renewed *Primary Framework* and the EYFS. It also met criteria which the government had laid down for commercial programmes offering 'high quality phonic work', which schools might be interested in purchasing.

The first of the six phases of the *Letters and Sounds* teaching programme begins in the EYFS and the final two, phases 5 and 6, take place throughout Years 1 and 2 respectively of KS1. Right at the beginning of the teaching programme, there is the following acknowledgment set off from the text in a separate box:

Enjoying and sharing books

Experience shows that children benefit hugely by exposure to books from an early age.

Right from the start, lots of opportunities should be provided for children to engage with books that fire their imagination and interest. They should be encouraged to choose and peruse books freely as well as sharing them when read by an adult.

Enjoying and sharing books leads to children seeing them as a source of pleasure and interest and motivates them to value reading.

(*Letters and Sounds: Six-phase Teaching Programme*, p. 2)

The *Notes of Guidance for Practitioners and Teachers* accompanying *Letters and Sounds* also acknowledge that 'Phonics is a means to an end. Systematic, high quality phonics teaching is essential, but more is needed for children to achieve the goal of reading, which is comprehension'. Practitioners and teachers are reminded that 'children need to understand the purpose of learning phonics and have lots of opportunities to apply their developing skills in interesting and engaging reading and writing activities' (p. 3). However, *Letters and Sounds* is purely concerned with phonics teaching and word recognition skills, so comprehension strategies are not even mentioned until Phase 6 and there are no activities to develop them. Phase 6 is described as where 'the shift from learning to read to reading to learn takes place and children read for information and pleasure' and it is stressed here that children should continue to be read to aloud so that 'they develop a love of reading' (*Six-phase Teaching Programme*, pp. 168–169).

Action Point

In the role of English subject leader, prepare a short report to a staff meeting arguing that the development of reading for pleasure and of positive attitudes to reading are important parts of the teaching of early reading. Use evidence from some of the official documents mentioned above to make your case. Anticipate difficult questions and objections to your argument and try to have answers ready to counter these.

Phonics and Reading for Pleasure

The UK government's guidance clearly acknowledges that phonics, of whatever sort, though essential, is not the whole of reading teaching. As Morag Stuart, one of the advisers to the 'Rose Review' of early reading, acknowledges: 'Reading the words is a necessary but not a sufficient condition for the understanding of written texts to take place' (Lewis and Ellis, 2006: 23). Teachers need to develop comprehension and reading for meaning as well as word recognition skills from the outset and need to make sure that positive attitudes are promoted through children's own independent experiences of reading and through being read to by adult readers. All this needs to take place within the context of a broad and rich language and literacy curriculum based on existing good early years practice. This will go some way to calming the fears of those teachers who were worried that a synthetic phonics approach, followed zealously, meant that children were not allowed near 'real books' until the programme was completed and were therefore restricted to artificial, phonically regular reading books until then.

The Rose Review itself comments: 'There is no doubt, too, that the simple text in some recognised favourite children's books can fulfil much the same function as that of decodable books. Thus it may be possible to use these texts in parallel, or in place of them' (DfES, 2006b: 27). The challenge for teachers, though, is clearly *how* to integrate an intensive and systematic programme of phonics teaching, where the expectation is that most children will know all the basic sounds of letters by the end of EYFS and have completed their phonic knowledge by the end of Year 1, within a broader reading curriculum. How can 'fidelity to the programme', whether government or commercial, which is stressed as essential to systematic phonics teaching, be combined with wider reading of imaginative children's literature? How can the very best children's books, which are not written to be phonically regular, be enjoyed by children who are being exposed only to phonically decodable texts in their teaching programme? In short, how can teachers make sure that a more rigorous and faster-paced phonics programme does not produce young readers who are proficient decoders but who are turned off reading? For, as Michael Rosen has warned:

> Those children who have already been convinced that reading a whole book will be a great thing to do (probably by their parents reading to them) will have little or no problem making the leap from phonics to real books and staying with them. For the millions of others who aren't convinced that reading is interesting or cool, no matter how good they are with their phonics, it's not clear why or how they will want to stick with it. (Lewis and Ellis, 2006: 124)

The schools described below have responded to the challenge of promoting the enjoyment of books and reading, at the same time as implementing the recommended systematic phonics teaching, in different ways. The first school mentioned has purchased a commercial synthetic phonics scheme but intends to use this in a particular way in conjunction with 'real books'.

Case Study School

In response to government initiatives on early reading, this primary school was planning to introduce Ruth Miskin's *Read Write Inc*, a commercial phonics scheme, into KS1 and then extend it later into KS2 for those older pupils still not secure with phonic knowledge. However, the English subject leader did not want the scheme to be used too prescriptively for reading teaching in the school, and wanted to make sure that the speaking and listening and writing elements in the scheme were properly covered too. 'It's very promising what they say you can achieve if you start it straightaway', she commented, 'but I was a bit worried that ordinary reading would go out of the window, because all the books are totally phonic … they're not a good read … some of them are actually quite funny!' However, this teacher felt she could still be creative and use her own ideas as well as use a systematic programme. In order to preserve wider reading and to encourage reading for pleasure, she had devised a way of combining 'real books' with 'scheme books': 'What we've decided to do is to give out ordinary paperback books, picture books, as reading material to take home rather than a reading scheme book … Bookmarks with advice on how parents can support children's reading for enjoyment will be sent home with them. The scheme books will remain in school to be used during literacy lessons.'

The second school has decided not to change its current multi-strategy approach to reading since it sees its existing practice as meeting the requirement to deliver high quality phonics teaching within a broad and rich language curriculum.

Case Study School

This infant school continues to encourage children to use a range of strategies to make sense of what they read, whether in whole class, group, paired or independent reading, and carefully monitors their progress in doing this. Though it is committed to phonics instruction, using a 'play' approach, this is not taught in isolation because of the dangers of children becoming over-reliant on one strategy. The school's aim is to get children to love books and to hook them into reading as early as possible, so there is never any suggestion that children must have a certain level of phonic knowledge before they are given free access to books. From the Reception classes onwards, as well as following a systematic phonics programme, the children are immersed in stories, using puppets and role-playing to re-enact them, and have a classroom library where they are allowed to choose books to read independently, with adults available to help if needed.

In the third school, there is an existing focus on introducing children to authors and their books in a systematic way, which will be continued and developed alongside the new requirements for teaching early reading.

Case Study School

This nursery and infant school has devised a way of ensuring that children experience a core of leading children's authors and their books during their time in the school. Each half-term from the nursery through to Year 2, every class focuses on an author who is particularly appropriate for reading aloud at that stage. There are displays on the chosen authors in each classroom and a collection of as many of their books as possible, which is stored centrally until needed. The class sets of books have two or three copies of each title, and other copies are available in the school library and on the bookracks in the classrooms. The aim is to generate interest in and enthusiasm for these writers, so that children want to borrow other books by them to take and share at home. By the end of KS1, each child will have detailed knowledge and experience of at least 12 authors. They can build on this experience by reading other books by similar authors who are recommended. The school intends to invest further to update and extend its author collections over the next few years.

Ways of Promoting Reading for Pleasure

Research quoted in Chapter 1 emphasised the elements of effective classroom practice in nurturing children's love of reading which tend to appear in successful schools such as those above:

- an enthusiastic reading teacher;
- activities that are open and authentic;
- a reading environment where there is easy access to plenty of suitable texts;
- pupil choice;
- collaborative learning;
- an approach where pupils are aware of what they are doing and how and why they are doing it;
- links between reading inside and outside the classroom, showing how readers in the world beyond the school also read for pleasure as well as for a variety of other purposes in their daily lives.

One element that is difficult to transfer from successful schools to others, without a change of personnel, is obviously an enthusiastic reading teacher. The other elements are more easily transferable and can be illustrated by ways in which successful nursery and infant teachers promote enjoyment of reading with young children. There is inevitably some overlap between the six categories.

Activities that are open and authentic

Classroom activities are most effective in enthusing children about reading where they are open-ended and have a real sense of purpose to them, rather than being artificial and closed-off tasks such as the completion of textbook exercises or worksheets. For example:

- **Arranging regular author and illustrator visits.** Any visit by a writer whose work children know and enjoy is valuable. However, the visit will be far more effective in promoting reading for pleasure if there is plenty of preparation beforehand. Reading and talking about the author's books are obviously fundamental, but there are other practical activities that can focus young children's reactions to their reading. For example, groups of children can fill a shoebox with objects based on their responses to a book or character before the author visits. These can be displayed before the visit, then shown to the writer and discussed on the day of the visit. Children can add to the boxes after the visit if there are other things that have suggested themselves during the writer's reading and talk.
- **Organising whole-school book or author days.** These can be effective ways of involving both pupils and parents in enjoyable and meaningful reading and writing activities. For example, Pam Craig (2006) describes the 'Katie Morag Days' organised in the school hall at a First School (4–9 years) over two days. Starting with a shared reading of Mairi Hedderwick's picturebook *Katie Morag and the Wedding* (1995), the days involved children, parents, grandparents and carers in a variety of activities related to the story, including role-playing in a corner transformed into Struay Post Office, as featured in the book. The Katie Morag days had the added benefit of allowing the adults to observe 'how to make the most of sharing a book with their children' (p. 19).
- **Swapping class reading recommendations with other schools via the Internet, or children making individual recommendations to 'keypals' in other schools.** Having a real audience and purpose for book recommendations, other than the immediate classroom context, is motivating for young readers. The Internet, properly supervised, provides a setting where children can communicate with other pupils they do not know personally in a direct and informal way. Sharing the pleasures of reading with others always adds to the enjoyment.
- **Keeping a class reading journal.** This needs to be easy for children to access for reference and for adding their own contributions. It could be kept in the reading area or the book corner of the classroom and can be a simple ring binder containing comments and drawings children have made in response to books read together as a whole class. Alternatively, the children's comments and pictures could be presented as a wall display, which is regularly updated to reflect books recently read aloud.
- **Arranging for children to create presentations based on stories or poems read, using props and costumes or glove puppets.** Children's enjoyment of stories and rhymes naturally expresses itself in play. Retelling

familiar narratives using simple theatrical resources such as masks or hand puppets enables pupils to communicate their enjoyment to others. It also gives them insights into book language, characters and story structure which can increase their pleasure in the texts performed.

- **Organising whole class 'choral reading' of poems.** This builds on children's instinctive enjoyment of music and song, since they work as a kind of choir to perform poems. The texts can be divided up into parts for soloists and parts for the whole ensemble, parts that are soft and parts that are loud, and so on, to follow the musical analogy. Each choral reading will be a slightly different interpretation of the poem, as with a musical performance, but can be taped and then enjoyed again.

A reading environment where there is easy access to plenty of suitable texts

Another common thread in schools that successfully promote reading is the provision of a print-rich environment and a range of interesting books and other reading materials which are updated regularly and which teachers are familiar with. This is just as crucial in the early years as for older readers, if not more so. Anyone who has tried to interest young children in reading will be aware of just how diverse their preferences are. What works with one child can fall completely flat with another. The only way to deal with this is to have as much suitable reading material available as possible, so that there is something to suit most tastes. However, an effective reading for pleasure environment is not just one that is flooded with books, as in the famous Bradford Book Flood experiment (Ingham, 1982), but one where children are guided towards what they are likely to enjoy, while still being able to chose for themselves.

Lessons from the children

Sometimes the children's drawings in my Reading Survey suggested how some pupils who feel reasonably positive about reading can feel daunted by the sheer number of books they feel they have to read, so that the bookshelf becomes almost a hurdle they have to jump, as in the drawing in Figure 3.1. Over-emphasis on targets, whether numbers of pages or books read or speed of reading, at the expense of enjoyment, can certainly impact on reading engagement in this way.

Examples of effective practice in creating rich reading environments for young children, which are not intimidating, might be:

- **Creating bookshops, newsagents or catalogue shops in the 'home corner' to encourage role-play reading and talk about fiction and non-fiction texts.** Usually the 'home corner' of the EYFS or KS1 classroom, whether it is set up as an estate agent's office, airport check-in desk or some other scenario, includes opportunities for developing literacy through play, but

Figure 3.1   Children can feel intimidated by the number of books they think they have to get through.

there is no reason why reading cannot be made the main focus. This can provide a context for children to experience different sorts of reading, both for pleasure and for a purpose, and to explore a wide range of reading material, which includes fiction but is not confined to it.

- **Making sure classroom libraries are easy for children to borrow from and that procedures for borrowing are clearly displayed.** Classroom book corners are not always inviting places and it is often not obvious how they are meant to be used. All children can be involved in looking after these sometimes neglected areas, and in making and keeping the class library a tidy, attractive place. They can design and put up information posters, label shelves and display books effectively, and take it in turns to be the 'librarians' who monitor borrowing and returning.
- **Involving the local SLS in auditing and stocking classroom libraries as well as the school library.** Occasional professional support as well as regular volunteer help is needed to make the most of school book collections. An SLS librarian can look at school book provision as a whole and at how

classroom and central book stocks fit together. Ideally, the classroom and school libraries should complement each other, but in practice classroom libraries are often ad hoc collections, containing teachers' own books or discarded school library books.

- **Each class 'adopting' an author and finding as many of her/his books as possible for the classroom.** Walking around primary schools today, it is not unusual to find classes or groups named after authors, whether Shakespeare and Dickens, Tolkien and Pullman, or Quentin Blake and Shirley Hughes. This can be taken one step further by a class or teaching group 'adopting' an author and becoming 'experts' in his or her work over a term or half-term. This involves the children finding out as much about the chosen writer as they are able, reading as much of their work as they can, and corresponding with the writer, if possible. They can then share their expertise and enthusiasm for their author in presentations to other classes or groups.

- **Having appetite-whetting displays of 'author of the month', 'book of the week' or 'poem of the day'.** These can easily be put together using posters, A3 copies of poems, or enlarged colour copies of book covers, along with children's comments about the texts. Other adults in the school and local community can take it in turns to contribute to the displays as well as teaching staff. Once the displays have become a regular and looked-for feature, children can contribute material or design the presentations as well. Once taken down, the display material will quickly build into an archive of information about writers and texts which makes a useful resource for classroom work.

- **Including bilingual picture book texts in school and classroom libraries.** A rich and inclusive reading for pleasure environment needs to include dual language texts such as picture books. These are particularly suited to bilingual editions because the pictures themselves provide an international language to support the written texts. These books are a valuable addition to the reading environment for monolingual readers as well as bilingual. Reading familiar words and pictures alongside an unfamiliar script gives children an insight into other languages and reading practices, often very different from their own. They can also appreciate that, though reading may be practised differently in different scripts, reading for pleasure is universal.

- **Having electronic books available on computers in the classroom.** Electronic books in this context are computer programs, usually on CD-ROM, which present text to children with an option to hear it read aloud, along with sound effects, music, hot spots to click on, and animations. This software enables children to decide on the amount of assistance they need for reading a text, either listening to the whole book, using the voice facility only when stuck on a word, or a level of support somewhere in between. This situation gives children the pleasure of 'reading' a book independently when their reading ability may make this difficult otherwise, with resultant gains in confidence, enjoyment and motivation. Using headphones for listening makes the experience even more like 'silent reading' for children working alongside other more competent readers.

Pupil choice

In effective approaches to promoting reading, children themselves are involved or consulted on a regular basis, not just as a one-off exercise. Research repeatedly shows that allowing pupils to take the lead, giving them genuine independence and autonomy in their decision-making about books and reading, where appropriate, increases engagement in the activity. There is no surprise in this; as adults, we are always more committed to activities we have a stake in, than to ones in which we have no say.

Examples of activities that promote pupil choice might be:

• **Providing plenty of opportunities for young children to read or browse books of their own choosing, independently.** Anyone who has watched young children sitting on the carpet of a bookshop absorbed in reading what they have just pulled off the bottom shelf of the children's section (often not the book the parent eventually buys) will appreciate the importance of children having the opportunity to choose freely. The freedom simply to open the book that catches your eye and see what is inside is fundamental to reading enjoyment. This freedom does not, of course, preclude giving children regular guidance, modelling book-selection for them and monitoring their independent reading choices.

• **Involving more able, independent readers in reading out their favourite short poems or stories as part of a '5-a-day' healthy reading campaign.** Children themselves make the best advocates for reading, so encouraging avid readers to share 'favourite bits' with their classmates during odd moments in the day has a cumulative effect of spreading enthusiasm to others. Finding five occasions in the primary school day to enjoy reading can be a tall order without this sort of pupil involvement, which also ticks boxes in speaking and listening development.

• **Asking children to bring in their own favourite books to go on a classroom 'reading for enjoyment bookshelf' for reading aloud or silent reading sessions.** As well as children bringing in and reading their favourites aloud, they can add their choices, temporarily, to a special bookshelf reserved for 'books we like to read'. If the bookshelf is used for individual reading, rather than reading aloud by the teacher, it can include other reading material as well as fiction, poetry and picture books.

• **Discussing children's reading choices and reflecting these when updating book stocks.** Building up a bookshelf of favourite reads, and comparing these with what is available in the classroom library, naturally leads to discussion about what children like or do not like to read and why. This in turn can lead to compiling a 'wish list' of reading material to refer to when ordering new stock.

• **Organising cross-curricular story-reading mornings, or whole days, when children can choose which stories they would like to hear.** These sessions can be organised around a theme or topic which the children are following. Each teacher can offer a different story suitable for a wide age-range and children can 'sign up' to the ones they would like to hear. Children could also suggest stories that they would like the teachers to read on the 'Story Morning'.

Collaborative learning

Reading is an activity that can be intensely private and also highly social, and for most readers it is both at different times. The benefits to pupils' learning of working together are well established: there are cognitive gains as well as social and emotional ones. As far as reading is concerned, collaborative reading-related activities increase motivation and promote more positive attitudes.

Lessons from the children

Reading with friends was important for the children in my Reading Survey. They usually reported enjoying collaboration in reading activities. As one contributor succinctly put it:

- *When you read with someone, it's better.*

Whereas another respondent complained:

- *It's unfair because all my friends go with each other in reading groups with no adult, but I have to go with an adult and I've only got one friend.*

Collaboration for pupils can be with peers, but also with younger or older partners. For example:

- **Using a 'Reading Buddies' scheme to pair experienced and inexperienced readers within the school or between schools.** This probably works best with volunteers, either older primary children from the same school or pupils from a nearby secondary school. When children are press-ganged into being 'buddies', it can become a chore which both partners resent. When the 'buddying' is in the right spirit, it works as a genuine partnership which has benefits for both the expert reader and the apprentice. It also needs to be a regular event if the partnership is to flourish, and both partners need training in how to make it successful. 'Buddying' between schools can also take place virtually, at least part of the time, using email and the Internet.
- **Using drama strategies such as group role-play and freeze frame to explore texts and responses.** Young children can use drama in a more exploratory way to investigate what they have read and to interact with it, as well as to present and perform texts. Activities such as collaborative role-play, improvisation, or presenting a series of freeze frames will require group negotiation of meanings and discussion of character, action and setting, which can enrich the reading experience.
- **Using electronic books and audio books in pairs or small groups.** Electronic books can be read collaboratively in addition to individually, allowing interaction between pupils as well as between pupils and text. Audio books can also be used by pairs or groups of children who can follow the text using multiple copies, making the reading experience more of a communal one. Children usually enjoy this social context for reading and feel in control of the

situation, since they can stop and start the reading when they wish. The group reading experience also encourages the sharing of ideas and responses.

- **Working together with older primary pupils to create picture books.** Young children can act as consultants, co-authors and audience for picture books created by older children. For example, at the design stage they can offer their views on what makes a good picture book and what their preferences are. They can also collaborate with the older pupils on selecting an appropriate title and cover, and make suggestions for the text or pictures. Early versions of the books can be trialled with the young audience. Finally, the finished picture books can be shared aloud with the young readers by their authors, and then placed in the classroom library for independent reading. Each book can have a comments page, where readers record their thoughts about the book.

An approach where pupils are aware of what they are doing and how and why they are doing it

Metacognition, or knowledge about knowledge, also has many benefits for promoting engagement with learning, including reading. Although the pleasures of reading may not be fully susceptible to rational analysis, it is important for young children to be aware of why and how we read. Adult leisure reading, after all, is usually first experienced by children as a silent and slightly mysterious activity. Studies of struggling readers report that they often show a lack of understanding of the point of reading, and the fact that people can derive pleasure from it, since no one has ever explicitly discussed this with them in addition to implicitly modelling it (Martin, 1989).

Ways to develop greater awareness might include:

- **Brainstorming ideas about 'what is reading for?'** Children can discuss this question first with a talk partner, before pooling their ideas. They usually need to be prompted to think about all the different ways we use reading in daily life, including for relaxation, escape or sheer enjoyment. Another way to approach the topic is to ask: 'What would be different in our daily lives if we couldn't read?'
- **Looking at non-fiction and a range of other forms of reading, including comics, magazines, newspapers and electronic texts, and discussing why and how we read them in different ways.** This discussion would follow naturally from the brainstorming activity above. As well as *how* and *why* we read the many different kinds of material we consume every day, the children could also discuss *when* and *where* they read certain kinds of texts.
- **Interviewing groups of children about books they read, at home and at school, and discussing their changing tastes and preferences.** As well as raising children's awareness of themselves as readers and their reading histories, these group interviews can contribute significantly to teachers' records of individual pupils if carried out regularly, say once a term. Children usually enjoy the opportunity to talk about their reading in situations where they do not feel pressurised to read aloud in front of others for assessment purposes.

- **Discussing the popularity of current children's bestsellers**, (e.g. The *Gruffalo* series by Julia Donaldson and Axel Scheffler). Why do some books sell by the million? Is their popularity to do with word of mouth recommendation, television book programmes, authors' names, covers, titles, book awards, reviews or other factors? Children can first research which books are most popular with their age group by conducting a classroom poll or by looking at some of the websites about children's books listed in the Resources section on page 126. The most popular books can then be shared aloud so that children can reflect on the qualities the texts have which have made them bestsellers, or on other factors involved, such as marketing or film and TV tie-ins.

- **Carrying out surveys of how children use their leisure time and what part reading plays in it.** Pupils and their parents can fill in a simple table to record how the children spend their evening or weekend on a chosen census day. The tables can be completed anonymously to avoid any embarrassment to pupils. They can record how much time is spent on reading school books, other books, comics and magazines, and how much on watching TV, videos or DVDs, and on computer use. Results can be collated and displayed in a bar chart.

- **Planning a poster campaign to promote their school as a 'Reading School'.** Year 2 children can be involved in designing and producing posters of different sizes to try to persuade the whole school community to read for pleasure at least once each day. They can then survey the school premises and decide on the best sites for displaying their campaign posters to reach their target audience, for example the dining hall, the school foyer, the playground and so on.

Lessons from the children

Children's perceptions of the value of reading in my Reading Survey varied, but the majority who were positive about the activity felt that it provided an escape into another world.

- *Reading is an adventure.*
- *Reading takes you to a different place.*
- *I read to help myself sleep and for pure pleasure. I also read to get away from this world and dive into a different world.*
- *I read sometimes to get out of the real world or if I am unhappy.*
- *I think that reading is far better than watching telly because you get into a whole world of your own with stories. I've been to America, China and Japan in my stories!*

Reading was also valued as a form of relaxation and de-stressing, important at a time when the pressures on primary-age children, both in and out of school, are reported to be greater than ever before.

- *It's a good way to relax. And if something's on your mind it can change your feelings and get your mind off it.*
- *I like reading because the stories are good and it gives you a private space in your head.*

(Continued)

(Continued)

- *Great way to calm down if you're unhappy or stressed out.*
- *Reading is once in life where you have peace.*

Reading was seen by the children as important for emotional or imaginative development, as well as the occasional opportunity for some consumer research.

- *I like reading because it is a way for me to get to see things from another person's point of view!*
- *Books make my imagination go wild.*
- *The only bad thing about reading is when you finish a really good book you feel like you've lost part of yourself, but the feeling disappears when you find another good book!*
- *I like to read up about stuff I want.*

However, reading was also seen more functionally by some children as related to passing tests and succeeding at school.

- *Reading is important to people because when it comes to SATs you will need to understand what it means so you can answer things clearly and as fully as you can.*
- *If you start reading all the time, you will be reading adult books at 7–8 years old. It also can get you into grammar school instead of a not very good school.*
- *I think that reading helps you a lot in other subjects.*
- *I think reading is a very good thing so you can learn instead of using the Internet.*
- *You will get clever if you read.*

Many children also saw reading as important for getting a job and acquiring life skills.

- *Reading is important. If you can't read you won't get a good job. If you want to be a teacher you need to read and know the reading.*
- *When you are older, you will need to read for your job like a nurse. You will need to read because it has notes and what is the matter with people.*
- *I want to be an actor when I am older so reading helps because I am going to read loads of scripts.*
- *I'm reading now because I want to be a motorbiker.*
- *If you can read, you will get a better job than someone who doesn't like reading.*
- *I think everyone should be able to read, otherwise they might not be able to read a danger sign, say, and could get into jeopardy.*

Links between reading inside and outside the classroom

Children are also able to see the point of reading better if they can see it happening 'naturally' in the 'real world' beyond the classroom walls, the world of everyday work and leisure. Reluctant readers often show a lack of appreciation of the place of reading in daily life, equating books and reading with school literacy only and making few connections with their home or community literacies. These are readers who *can* read, but perceive reading as something they are forced to do in the classroom and will not choose to do once out of it.

Ways of making links for young children between reading in and out of school might include:

- **Taking children to the local library, where they can borrow a book to take home and later talk about in school.** This is perhaps the most direct way of making links with reading in the local community. It can also be an effective way of involving parents in their children's reading development, since they can be invited along as well and will need to sign library membership forms where necessary. Alternatively, the library can be brought to the school by inviting the local children's librarian to talk to pupils about becoming members, or arranging a visit by the mobile library van if there is no branch library nearby.
- **Making links with a local bookseller to arrange two-way visits and to organise regular bookselling in the school.** After the local library, this is the next most obvious way to make connections with the reading community outside the school gates. Children can visit the bookshop, if nearby, in small groups to see how it operates, how staff display books in order to attract interest, how they shelve them, what happens to books that are not sold, and so on. The bookseller can arrange to visit after school to make a range of children's books available to parents and children who might not usually buy books.
- **Inviting parents and grandparents into the classroom to talk about and share their favourite childhood reading.** Parents and grandparents can make effective reading advocates. Inviting those who are keen readers and good communicators to talk to pupils about the books they read when they were the same age helps to spread their enthusiasm and interest to other children as well as their own. They can also read aloud some of their best-loved stories and rhymes.
- **Arranging for members of the non-teaching staff to bring in and talk about a typical week's reading material for work and leisure.** Avid readers who are members of the school's non-teaching staff can also be recruited as promoters of reading. Children are usually pleasantly surprised to see and hear about the range and quantity of a typical week's work and leisure reading for a keen adult reader who is not a teacher (teachers are assumed, rightly or wrongly, to read all the time as part of their job!). This is an effective and easy way to give children an insight into everyday reading practices that take place outside of the school curriculum.
- **Using a reading mascot: children listen to a story and can then choose to take the book home along with the mascot, usually a cuddly toy.** The children can read or listen to the story at home with the reading mascot, possibly share other books with the mascot, then bring it back and

talk to the other children about the reading they have done. The mascot can keep a reading diary, recording all the stories read to it and what it enjoyed about each one.

- **Taking children to reading events at a local literature festival.** Like reading groups, literary festivals have become more and more popular and widespread in the UK in recent years, ranging from events in large cities sponsored by national newspapers, lasting two weeks or more, to shorter affairs in local communities, often organised by libraries, book groups, or sometimes clusters of schools themselves. Most literature festivals include a programme of children's book events, often with free sessions for local schools. Details of regular festivals can be found at www.britishcouncil. org/arts-literature-literary-festivals.htm

- **Inviting storytellers from the local community to perform in school.** Listening to oral storytelling done well can have a positive effect on children's engagement with reading. When children have experienced the power and excitement of, say, folk tales from oral performances, they are much more motivated to seek out and enjoy the written forms of these narratives. Storytelling is another cultural practice that has grown in popularity in recent years and there are professional or amateur storytellers in many local communities. The Society for Storytelling's website (www.sfs.org.uk), which is searchable by region, gives a directory of UK storytellers whose performances have been well received. The website also gives details of National Storytelling Week, which the Society organises at the end of January and beginning of February each year.

- **Getting children to take part in or shadow national television book competitions.** For example the Blue Peter Children's Book Awards, which have three categories, 'Best Book with Facts', 'Best Illustrated Book to Read Aloud' and 'The Book I Couldn't Put Down' (www.bbc.co.uk/cbbc/blue-peter/bookclub). Children's books are not often featured on mainstream British television, but where they are, as in this example or occasionally in the 'Richard and Judy' book programme (www.richardandjudybookclub. co.uk), there is an opportunity to tap into the excitement and glamour generated by TV, which is part of children's daily experience out of school, in order to promote reading for enjoyment.

Action Point

List three innovations based on the case study schools and examples of good classroom practice given above which you could introduce into your own teaching, or your school's overall practice, to improve provision for promoting reading at EYFS or KS1. Put them in order of priority.

Reading for Pleasure across the Curriculum

This has two aspects:

- using children's enjoyment of literature in other subject areas, outside of literacy lessons, to promote learning in those areas;
- extending children's enjoyment of reading to include non-literary texts in other subject areas.

Children's enjoyment of literary reading does not have to end with the literacy lesson. Stories and poems offer ways into other areas of learning for young children. It is important, though, that the literature used is worth reading in its own right. A picture book may offer attractive links to the topic being studied, but if it does not have an engaging storyline and illustrations that capture children's attention then using it will be counterproductive. Using poor-quality books in any context gives the unspoken message that the reading experience does not really matter. Cross-curricular projects can be organised around good-quality picture books. For example, *The Lighthouse Keeper's Lunch* by Ronda and David Armitage (1977), as well as being an enjoyable and worthwhile read in itself, invites problem-solving activities in other curriculum areas such as Science or Design and Technology (how to get lunch to the lighthouse keeper without the seagulls eating it). Adequate time needs to be allowed, though, for reading and enjoying stories or poems like these which are used in other subject areas.

Familiar stories or rhymes and traditional tales can also be revisited in cross-curricular contexts. Looking at these stories from a different angle can enhance children's pleasure in hearing them again, or, in an increasing number of cases, actually hearing the stories for the first time.

Case Study School

This infant and nursery school has organised learning at KS1 into a topic-based curriculum since well before the publication of the government's *Excellence and Enjoyment* document (DfES, 2003), which promoted this approach. The teachers use fairy tales such as *The Three Little Pigs, Jack and the Beanstalk* and *The Elves and the Shoemaker* to link Literacy with Design and Technology and with Science; for example, looking at materials, plant growth or evaluating footwear. These particular tales were chosen in part because they were seen as boy-friendly stories. Another topic on castles, also seen as having boy-appeal, was linked with the reading of Ruth Brown's classic atmospheric picture book *A Dark, Dark Tale* (1981). The construction of a castle in the classroom 'home corner' gave plenty of opportunities for role-playing related to this text. Other stories used across the curriculum in this way are also acted out using simple props and dressing up clothes, or alternatively using puppets that the children have made themselves based on characters in the books read.

Nurturing a love of reading in children should not be confined to literary texts such as fiction, playscripts and poetry. Children should take pleasure in reading non-literary and non-fiction texts, as well as reading them for a purpose, such as information retrieval. Most children, of course, do enjoy reading both fiction and non-fiction. In my own research on what children read at home, parents reported that a large majority (87%) of their children who enjoyed reading fiction also enjoyed non-fiction. As discussed earlier, for some children, particularly boys, non-fiction reading is actually their preferred type because it is the one which gives them most pleasure, whether it be *The Guinness Book of Records*, the *Eyewitness Guide* series, or a football magazine such as *Four-Four-Two*. In the same home reading surveys, parents reported that 72% of boys enjoyed non-fiction reading at home, compared with 57% of girls.

Lessons from the children:

In the pupils' own comments on their reading as part of my survey, almost two-thirds of the children reported enjoying non-fiction. The comments of some of the respondents, however, were a reminder that for a sizeable minority of pupils, with significantly more boys than girls, the pleasures of reading were confined to non-fiction books.

- *I like reading non-fiction books and maths books and I don't like fiction books and I like formulas like A + B = C.*
- *I LOVE non-fiction books.*
- *I like to read the non-fiction books on animals because I want to become a vet when I'm older and reading lots of information and facts about lots of animals will help a lot.*
- *Reading is boring except when it's about motorbikes or bikes.*
- *Instruction books (how to make things) are very fun.*

Promoting the pleasures of non-fiction reading, particularly for girls, a substantial minority of whom do not read it for enjoyment, can take various forms. Reading non-fiction books aloud to children is one of the simplest and most effective ways to do this. Many information books for younger children are written in narrative form, and these lend themselves to being read aloud like any other story. The popular *Read and Wonder* series, published by Walker Books, uses the resources of poetic language to make learning about topics a uniquely pleasurable reading experience. For example, in Mike Bostock's *Think of an Eel* (1993) from this series, readers find out about eels through the sounds, rhythm and imagery of the language used as well as the factual information that is given. The subtle and powerful language of these kinds of information books cries out to be read aloud and savoured.

But more conventional non-fiction texts can also be listened to and enjoyed. Here the reading will not be sequential, as with a narrative or poetic text. Reading aloud will model the behaviour of information book readers in focusing on particular pages through using contents and indexes. Listening to relevant pages of a well-written children's information book should be enjoyable and should give young children a feel for the cadences of non-fiction writing in different genres, which can inform their own writing. Asking children to bring in their own examples of enjoyable information books to share with others will help spread the word that non-fiction can be fun.

Many non-fiction books now use humour and a comic-strip format to engage children's interest. This approach was pioneered by Terry Deary in his *Horrible Histories* series and has been widely imitated, spreading to most other areas of the curriculum. Terry Deary's aim was quite simply to get children to enjoy reading non-fiction by using all the verbal and visual devices of a genre they already did read for pleasure and from choice, the comic book. Deary's books have their detractors, who feel they are not 'real' information books, despite the level of detail they usually contain about their subjects and the authentic sources they often use. However, there can be no doubting that Deary has achieved his aim of getting children to realise that non-fiction reading need not be dull and boring. *Horrible Histories* and the like owe their success also to their direct address to the child audience, promoting themselves as books that deal with the parts of history the 'adults don't want you to read'. This makes them popular for children's own independent reading, but means they are less likely texts for reading aloud, bearing in mind the visual aspect of the books as well. However, some teachers do report using the books selectively as read alouds.

Reading for Pleasure on Screen

Again, there are a number of different aspects to this topic:

- recognising that reading multimedia texts on screen using various new technologies is a form of reading for enjoyment in its own right;
- recognising that these new technologies can enhance the enjoyment of more traditional texts rather than replace them;
- recognising that viewing or creating purely visual screen texts such as films can enhance the enjoyment of books and reading.

In the renewed *Primary Framework for Literacy* (DfES, 2006a), the reading and writing objectives all appear under the repeated heading 'Read and write for a range of purposes on paper and on screen', emphasising the importance now given in the curriculum to screen-based literacies. This reflects the part that these forms of reading and writing increasingly play in children's lives. From a very young age, children will be used to reading or listening to reading from a TV or computer screen; for example, parents often buy electronic toys to help their preschool children learn sounds. For older children, reading from the screen, whether mobile phone, iPod, palmtop or laptop PC, will be something they routinely do for enjoyment as well as information in their leisure time. Schools are beginning to recognise that these screen-based texts are a legitimate source of independent reading for pleasure in their own right, whether in the classroom during silent reading or as home reading to be recorded in a reading log. They also increasingly recognise that new technology can be used to promote more traditional literacies; for example, downloading the texts of poems onto MP3 players or watching and creating poetry performances online. One of the poet Michael Rosen's first ideas when appointed as Britain's Children's Laureate in 2007 was to set up a *You Tube*-style website for poetry performance, an idea inspired by his son.

In the school described below, the three aspects of screen reading listed above were combined in a visual literacy project for KS1 pupils based on a classic story and following objectives from the NLS.

Case Study School

Throughout the second half of the summer term, the Year 2 class in this primary school were reading an 'extended story', *The Wind in the Willows,* by a 'significant children's author', Kenneth Grahame, to use terms from the NLS. The teacher, who was the school's English subject leader, decided to use a screen adaptation of the classic story to enhance the children's enjoyment and appreciation of the novel and to develop their visual literacy, in this case their knowledge and understanding of film.

Phase one of the project began with the children listening to the soundtrack only of the opening few minutes from the screen version of the story. They used this to predict the settings, characters and mood of the story, before listening to the opening read aloud, discussing and enjoying the language used with the aid of an interactive whiteboard, and then viewing the story opening on DVD. In the second phase of the project, the children worked in small groups to act out pieces of dialogue and description from the middle part of the story where Mr Toad has a series of misadventures. They also investigated the different kinds of screen shots used in the film version of this section, and made voice-overs for clips from the DVD.

In groups, the children then used puppets, including ones they created themselves in Design and Technology sessions, to re-enact these central episodes from the story. They carried out a location search for suitable places round the school for filming one episode, and used a digital camera to take photographs of their puppets acting out this scene. These pictures were put into a sequence using Movie Maker software or PowerPoint.

The third and final phase of the project involved the children writing a sustained story based on the character of Mr Toad and his escapades in the middle part of *The Wind in the Willows*, and told in the first person. The story was presented for reading in either book or screen-based form.

Table 3.1 shows an extract from the detailed planning for phase 2 of the *Wind in the Willows* visual literacy project.

Table 3.1   *Extract from the planning for a project to enhance enjoyment of a classic text through developing film literacy*

Phase 2: Visual reading, speaking and listening	
Session Objectives: **Reading:** Look at the way that one event leads to another in *The Wind in the Willows*. Select extracts from the story that demonstrate cause and effect so that children can reread together. Ask children to give explanations of why things happen in the story. **Speaking and Listening:** Make voice-over for the Windows Movie Maker clips. **ICT**: Use microphone to record story alongside pictures.	
Teaching Sequence	**Activities** **Independent learning / Guided learning**
Children work in small groups to enact pieces of dialogue and improvise, using description rather than sound effects, e.g. *Suddenly Mole heard a cuckoo – he felt....*	Look closely at opening clips – what are the important parts that move the story on? Look at screen shots – give page of choices – close up, etc. Children guess how many changes of screen shot there are in first 5 minutes, then watch Identify, while watching, the various types of screen shot; can they say what effect the different shots have on the viewer? Answer why/ because statements Groups – teacher takes group 2 to tell story
ICT: use Windows Movie Maker project file *Wind in the Willows* 1.6. Children add spoken word	Children write commentary of sounds and feelings Whole class contribution of ideas collected to potentially add script to movie
Plenary Listen to retelling	
Phase 2: Speaking and listening/drama/writing	
Session Objectives: **Reading**: Discuss techniques used by Kenneth Grahame to sustain the reader's interest, for example cliff-hangers at the end of chapters. **Speaking and Listening**: Summarise the second part/ middle of the story. **Drama**: Use puppets to retell second part/middle of the story. **ICT**: Photograph puppets in various locations around school. **DT**: Make Ratty puppet.	

(Continued)

Table 3.1 *(Continued)*

Teaching Sequence	Activities Independent learning/Guided learning
Show structure of the story – Mr Toad likes new things, continues to take cars and then crashes	Group at a time go with Teaching Assistant to take photographs of Toad being chased and hiding
Mole and Ratty want to help *Where is Toad?*: this part of story to be recreated using puppets	
In pairs, retell the part where he is locked up and escapes	Teacher to put existing screen shot photographs on Windows Movie Maker
Groups of 4 take roles of different characters; plan some places around school where we could film the next part of the story	Show children how to put pictures into a sequence

If there is a problem use PowerPoint |
| **Plenary**
Show whole class process of Windows Movie Maker as a recap
Assessment criteria: children can work in a group and take roles to retell part of a story | |

Acknowledgement is due to Jill Woof for permission to reproduce this plan.

Involving Parents

As already discussed in Chapter 2, this is an important factor in promoting reading for enjoyment right across the primary phase. If every child matters, then clearly every parent matters. However, it is particularly crucial at the beginning of children's schooling in the EYFS and in KS1. This is because, firstly, it can set the pattern for parental support of reading both within school and at home which may continue throughout the primary years. It is clearly vital to get the partnership right at this stage:

> Because we know that older children who have more positive motivations towards reading have higher levels of reading achievement ... we need to do all we can to ensure that children's early home lives afford opportunities to develop such motivations. (Baker et al., 1997: 80)

Secondly, it is important that the right *sort* of parental engagement with children's reading is established at this early stage. Children are still mostly learning to read fluently and have not yet become independent readers. But, as discussed, they will be increasingly subject to intensive and schematic phonics teaching programmes within school. How schools train parents to balance support for the phonics programme at home with encouragement of the reading habit for its own sake will be a key factor. Research evidence points to the importance of parents being encouraged to emphasise the fun aspects of reading. As Baker et al. also point out:

> Parents who believe that reading is a source of entertainment have children with more positive views about reading than do parents who emphasize the skills aspect of reading development. These findings have important implications for offering guidance to parents and for the development of family literacy intervention programs. (p. 69)

Since the evidence also suggests that 'many children from low-income families do not grow up in homes that emphasize the entertainment value of reading' (p. 80), and that fathers when recruited into supporting reading at home are often more likely to insist on technical correctness, schools need to ensure that their training reaches those parents and carers with whom it is traditionally the hardest to form partnerships.

Lessons from the children

Some children in my pupil Reading Survey with negative views about reading reported strong parental pressure to read, particularly from mothers but occasionally from fathers.

- *My mum doesn't like it when I don't read.*
- *I wouldn't read unless my mum told me to.*
- *I don't like reading but my dad says it's good for me.*

This training for parents of early readers will need to make sure:

- That the mechanics of the school's approach to phonics teaching is clearly explained, so that parents can support this at home and do not use other conflicting schemes or approaches. For example, one primary school gives all first-time parents a take-home pack containing exercises and information based on phonic work done in the classroom. Another runs training courses for parents accredited by the Open College network to ensure consistency of approach in phonics with training given to teachers and teaching assistants.
- That parents understand the need to be patient and have realistic expectations of children's progress. Parents' anxieties about when their child will be moved on to the next stage or colour in a reading scheme soon communicate themselves to children. Well-intentioned parents often want to move their children on to longer and more demanding books before it is appropriate. As one teacher put it: 'There's this huge emphasis on

speedy progress and parents don't realise the true meaning of understanding a story. They say their son can tell me what happened, but he may not be able to infer anything at all. They want their child to be reading *The Hobbit* at 7'.

- That the main lesson children should learn at home is that reading is enjoyable and not another household chore.
- That reading at home does not have to be confined to the school reading book.
- That the emphasis should be on praise and encouragement, not negative criticism and over-correction of miscues.
- That discussion of books and reading beyond the level of what happens in the story is important.
- That listening to early readers is essential, but reading aloud to them and sharing the reading is also important.

One school tries to communicate these messages to parents through both whole school and individualised support meetings.

Case Study School

This primary school sees its partnership with parents as an interactive process where each partner can learn from and support the other. The school has a meeting for all new parents about reading, which includes answering questions from them about reading *and* taking ideas from parents about what they do at home to help children. Any parents who want to help in the classroom are recruited at this stage and given specific training for this role.

A reading log offers two-way communication with parents about their child's reading and is also used as a way of training them in how to help their child take the next step. Significant developments recorded in the logs are transferred to the teachers' own reading records. There are sets of guidance sheets for parents for different types of books, so they can support young readers in the right sort of way.

The school feels that time invested at this stage is well spent, so it follows up the meeting by offering one-to-one sessions and individualised training to help parents develop their children's reading. These sessions include teachers observing and supporting parents listening to their children read. The advice to parents here is to encourage their children to enjoy reading and not simply to correct their mistakes.

Action Point

Draft an agenda for a meeting with new parents about:

1. How reading is taught at EYFS or KS1 within your school.
2. How parents can support this approach through reading with their children at home.

Chapter 4

Promoting Reading for Pleasure in the Later Primary Years

Summary

Chapter 4 begins by discussing the renewed PNS *Primary Framework* for schools in England as it affects the development of reading for enjoyment with Key Stage 2 pupils (7–11 years). The use of whole texts with older primary children is then focused on, specifically novels, picture books and poems. The chapter includes examples of classroom-tested planning to illustrate good practice in the use of novels and poems with children in this age range. Using the same research-based headings as in Chapter 3, practical ways of promoting reading for pleasure are then suggested for use with KS2 children.

The renewed *Primary Framework for Literacy and Mathematics* (DfES, 2006a) signals a change of focus in teaching reading at the beginning of Key Stage 2 with the following statement: 'Year 3 (7–8 years) is a significant year for moving the emphasis on teaching from word recognition to language comprehension' (DfES, 2006a: 28). Clearly, this should only be a shifting of developmental priorities. Comprehension should have been nurtured since the beginning of learning to read, as discussed in the previous chapter; there cannot be a sudden lurch towards reading for meaning at the age of 7. To mark this boundary, strand 5, 'Word Recognition', disappears from the *Framework* after Year 2.

Progression in reading at KS2 is therefore measured in terms of strands 7 and 8 only, 'Understanding and interpreting texts' and 'Engaging with and responding to texts', which have of course already run throughout the Foundation Stage and KS1. Although there is some overlap between the two, strand 7 focuses more on the text and strand 8 on the reader. The summary of 'Understanding and interpreting texts' uses verbs such as 'retrieve, select and describe', 'deduce, infer and interpret', 'identify', 'explain and comment' (DfES, 2006a: 16). The strand involves developing an evidence-based approach to how different fiction and non-fiction texts and genres are structured, how they use language and style, and how effects on readers are produced. 'Engaging with and responding to texts', on the other hand, is summarised by verbs such as 'read', 'respond' and 'evaluate'. This strand is concerned with developing reader response, exploring personal preferences for books and authors, comparing themes in texts, and discussing books with other readers. This is the strand in the *Framework* which actually mentions enjoyment of reading: 'Read independently for purpose, pleasure and learning' (DfES, 2006a: 16).

Approaches to promoting reading for pleasure at KS2 will need to build on and develop those used at KS1. However, many of the general approaches and specific strategies used with young readers will still be relevant. There should be continuity alongside the progression to children becoming fully fledged independent readers with their own tastes and preferences. Older children should be encouraged to value the reading they did when younger, rather than to disown it or feel embarrassed about it now they are in the 'big' school. One practical way to encourage this attitude is to get KS2 pupils to make 'memory boxes' of favourite books from nursery and infant days and to give them time to revisit books and authors they remember enjoying. They can then choose old favourites to share with younger children in 'reading buddy' sessions. Part of the pleasure in reading at all ages is to re-read what is familiar and to pass on the enjoyment to others.

The *Framework* also signals the need for teachers of older KS2 pupils to support them in continuing to read for enjoyment during the transition to KS3. 'Core Learning in Literacy' includes a set of objectives for 'Year 6 progression to Year 7' with an accent on independent reading, exploring literary heritages, reading between the lines and appraising the value of texts. This section of the *Framework* is an important recognition of the role primary teachers can play as children move into secondary education, and not just in terms of the literacy curriculum. Parting gifts of suitable books for soon-to-be Year 7 readers, opportunities for Year 6 to donate name-plated books to the primary school library before leaving, and invitations for pupils to return during their Year 7 to take part in running reading-related clubs and activities are all ways of building bridges to span the transition to the period of their schooling when young people are most likely to lose the pleasure reading habit, sometimes for good. There is nothing more disheartening for a teacher than meeting former pupils who were avid readers at primary school and finding that what they have learnt, six months into their secondary school career, is that reading is not cool any more and the library is not a place to be seen in.

Using Whole Texts

The over-use of text extracts in literacy teaching at KS2 has come in for increasing criticism from teachers and others since the introduction of the Literacy Hour in primary schools in 1997–8. For example, the QCA consultation exercise *English 21* reported:

the overwhelming view [is] that reading whole novels, picture books and short stories is essential. Sustained narrative reading and reading for pleasure are high priorities. (QCA, 2005: 14)

Using short passages from texts to illustrate genre features, language use, comparisons of theme or style and so on, obviously has its place. But English subject leaders I interviewed as part of my research detected worrying cases of 'extractitis' in many older primary readers reared on a diet of text fragments, often covered in sticky notes, which were only slowly peeled back to reveal key words. Although this textual striptease may have inspired some children to go away and find the book from which the extract was taken, for most this approach to shared reading was a frustrating experience. I have seen many well-intentioned teachers and trainees, following the original NLS, read the opening of a story to enthralled children only to stop after a page and discuss the features of a good opening, moving on then to read another good story opening. Both stories would be left hanging in the air at the end of the lesson, as if a good opening could somehow be disassociated from the rest of the story. The satisfaction all readers need from hearing what happens next in a story and how it all ends was denied.

At KS1 it was easier for teachers to work with whole texts in the Literacy Hour since these tended to be short picture book texts. The more extended texts appropriate at KS2 were harder to fit into the structure of the Literacy Hour, combined with the detailed objectives and the short weekly planning units of the original NLS. As one teacher I interviewed put it, 'when my children come to me in Year 6 they very often have never read an entire book. They have read bits and pieces of it'.

Pause for Thought

What are the pros and cons of using whole texts or using extracts to generate interest in reading? When would it be more appropriate to use one or the other? How could the use of both whole texts and extracts be combined?

The renewed *Primary Framework* encourages longer units of literacy teaching, lasting up to five weeks, giving more scope for dealing with more substantial whole texts. The examples of long-term planning made available to teachers when the new *Framework* was introduced group the reduced number of learning objectives into three main themes: Narrative (including playscripts), Non-Fiction and Poetry. Each of these themes forms a block in medium-term planning and each block is divided into a number of units. For Year 5 and Year 6 pupils, 'additional text-based units' are suggested which are centred on specific, complete novel and poetry texts (www.standards.dfes.gov.uk/primary frameworks/literacy/planning).

This recommended approach to planning recognises the need, particularly with older KS2 pupils, to increase enjoyment by allowing readers sufficient time to engage with whole texts in sustained, varied and imaginative ways. The suggested activities provide frequent opportunities for drama and discussion, as well as for pupils' own writing, in response to the chosen texts, in line with the increased emphasis on the integration of speaking and listening, reading and writing activities in the renewed *Framework*. As one subject leader I interviewed for my research project said: 'Because it's a much less rigidly structured approach, that will allow me time for more discussion of books with children and hopefully we'll get a lot more depth'. However, as well as providing opportunities for teachers, shared whole-class reading of complete texts over a period of several weeks also poses challenges. As another interviewee confessed: 'Longer units look interesting, but quite scary to sustain over a long period'.

Teaching literacy through sustained text-based units of work is not new, of course. Many of the schools I visited for my research, which had successfully helped older primary children catch the reading bug, had continued to use this approach under the earlier NLS, using novels, picture books and poetry. Some examples from these schools featuring the three genres mentioned are discussed below.

Novels

Reading a whole novel takes time and there are no short cuts to take without defeating the object of the exercise. Traditionally, teachers read the class novel aloud to older primary pupils over a period of perhaps half a term, often at the end of the day. As mentioned in Chapter 2, this practice became much less common at KS2 after the implementation of the NLS, and, where it did continue, time constraints meant that frequently only a few pages were read in a week. The reading of the book often stretched out for a term or more, long after the pupils' interest in it had died.

What are the pleasures available to older primary pupils from reading longer fiction texts? The literacy demands on readers today are much more diverse than in even the recent past and are dominated by screen-based information and entertainment texts. Adults who read fiction regularly are in the minority. So should novel fiction retain its central place in the school literacy curriculum? As discussed elsewhere in this book, it is vital that older pupils and boys in particular be allowed a reading diet in the classroom that is varied and balanced, including electronic, non-fiction and non-literary texts. However, engagement with a sustained piece of narrative fiction offers unique pleasures and should still be an important part of rounded literacy provision.

Reading a good novel at KS2, particularly in a whole class context, offers, among other things:

- the satisfactions of following an extended plot over time;
- the experience of feeling empathy with a wide range of characters;

- the enjoyment of language used for sustained dialogue, action and description;
- the chance to appreciate a well-made, complex story structure;
- the pleasure of using the imagination to create pictures in the mind;
- the opportunity to share impressions and predictions with other readers.

Shared reading and talking about a novel can provide all these benefits. Other reading, writing, speaking and listening activities related to a sharing of the text *can* enhance the joys of novel reading, but can also be counter-productive if they are seen as dull or arbitrary tasks. Response activities of this type need not be unimaginative or unstructured, however. A theoretical back-bone is provided, for example, by Benton and Fox (1985: 13–16), who list 'four activities that comprise the basic elements of the process of responding':

- *Picturing*: the making of mental images.
- *Anticipating and retrospecting*: a continuous series of predictions and back-ward glances.
- *Interacting*: the reader projecting into the text his or her own experience.
- *Evaluating*: the valuing of a text, which goes on continuously as we read.

All these processes are present and interrelate in the act of reading a novel. Teachers can devise activities that highlight one or more of the elements of response, and encourage children not only to 'read the lines', but also to 'read between the lines', making inferences and deductions from what they read, and sometimes to 'read beyond the lines', making evaluations and justifying their own views. Benton and Fox (1985: 13–16) give as examples of such activities:

- *Picturing*: sketches of characters, places, incidents during reading; more considered pictures or collages to express overall responses after reading.
- *Anticipating and retrospecting*: a frieze of plot development for display in the classroom, updated after each reading. Diaries and letters written in role as characters.
- *Interacting*: drama activities such as improvisation, role-play and freeze frame activities, which allow children to put themselves in the action of a novel and make the action relevant to them; writing new episodes using the same characters or settings.
- *Evaluating*: planning an advertising campaign for a novel; writing an email to the author giving reactions to a novel.

In the case study school discussed below, KS2 children were exposed to as much reading of whole narrative texts as possible in order to help them dis-cover the pleasures of fiction reading. As well as having a class novel that was read aloud each day, the children had a story time at the end of the day, a complete text for a guided group reading session each week, and read a whole novel text, alongside related activities, as part of a number of planned units of work in literacy which ran over several weeks.

Case Study School

This junior school believes strongly in reading a whole book. The English subject leader feels that many schools are coming around to this way of thinking, as literacy teaching evolves from the previous 'death by extracts'. The school also believes in choosing texts which both teachers and pupils can enjoy. The teachers plan units of work around three or four whole books in each year group. With Year 4, for example, this currently involves books such as *The Butterfly Lion* by Michael Morpurgo, *The Iron Man* by Ted Hughes, *The Ice Palace* by Robert Swindells and *Grandpa Chatterji* by Jamila Gavin. The teachers tend to pick books that are well-resourced and have clear cross-curricular links. So *Grandpa Chatterji* fits in with current topics in geography and religious education such as India and Hinduism.

For the subject leader, this approach makes class reading more real and enjoyable for the children and ensures that all have the experience of finishing a complete novel: 'There will be children in all schools, no matter how much you work hard to promote reading, especially the lower ability children, that might not finish a whole book. So the weaker readers have an opportunity to listen to a whole book. It's wonderful for them.' He also feels that sharing whole books in this way has benefits for children's writing, again for the less able writers in particular. Children have sustained opportunities to hear the cadences and vocabulary of narrative writing, to internalise these and reproduce them in their own writing. For him, this is more effective in improving writing than decontextualised 'feature-spotting'.

Table 4.1 shows an extract from the planning for a three-week unit on the novel *The Butterfly Lion* with Year 4 children in this case study school. The extract covers the three days available in the first week of the unit and was produced to meet the objectives of the original NLS framework. The text is introduced during this first week by reading aloud a substantial part of the novel, which is continued in the separate story time slot, and by providing some background context for the author and the book. Alongside this input from the teacher, there are opportunities for drawing, writing in role, discussion and reflection by the children, working in pairs, small groups or as a whole class. These activities allow them to engage in the response processes mentioned by Benton and Fox (1985) above of *picturing* (designing a front cover), *anticipating and retrospecting* (the 60-second challenge), *interacting* (hot seating, conscience alley and writing letters in role), and *evaluating* (comparing front covers, sharing responses to the chapters read).

Picture books for older children

Picture books also have their place as whole texts to be shared at KS2. This is another area of continuity and progression after KS1. After an initial resistance by some children to going back to 'baby books', which they identify with learning to read, KS2 readers soon rediscover the particular pleasures offered to independent readers by these mixed media texts. As well as being part of a balanced reading diet for those KS2 children who already read for

Table 4.1 *Extract from the planning for a sustained, three-week teaching unit on a complete novel text*

Literacy Weekly Planner for Year Group 4

Context (Stimulus): *The Butterfly Lion* **by Michael Morpurgo T1** To identify social, moral or cultural issues. **T8** To write critically about an issue or a dilemma raised in a story, explaining the problem, alternative courses of action and evaluating the writer's solution.

Success Criteria: (see below)

	Speaking and Listening Activities	Thinking Hat Activities	Demonstration Writing Activities	Guided Writing Activities	
	Whole Class Work		**Independent/Guided Work**	**Plenary**	**Assessment opportunities**
Monday **Ch 1 & 2** **MG to read** **Ch 3 during story time**	**T1 T8** Start off by asking the children if they have heard of Michael Morpurgo. Get the children to work with their talk partners and discuss which books by MM they know. List these and explain that he often writes books about his own experiences and historical books. Read the blurb to the children and show them the front cover. Ask the children why the book is called *The Butterfly Lion*. Share their ideas. Read the first chapter and discuss why the boy didn't like public school. Discuss what 'homesick' is and if the children have ever felt like this. Have the children ever felt like running away? Read the second chapter and ask the class whether they would go ever go away with a stranger. As the story develops discuss what a 'compound' is and ask children where lions might be found. Ask the children what they think the 'veld' is and what it looks like, based on what the author has told them. Also how life seemed to be different for men and women (men had exciting adventures on the veld, women stayed home with the children in the compound). Could also pick up on foreign words. Explain to the children that they are going to design a front cover to *The Butterfly Lion*. Model ideas.		Give out copies of the book with different front covers and ask the children which one they prefer. Share responses. Children to create a front cover for the book in groups. MG with Guided Writing group Resources – **copies of *The Butterfly Lion*. Writing frame for book.**	Hot seat the boy in the first chapter. Encourage the children to ask him questions about boarding school and why he ran way.	Children are able to create a front cover for *The Butterfly Lion*.

Table 4.1   (Continued)

Wednesday **Ch 4 & 5** **Read Ch 6** **during** **story time**	**T1 T8** Ask the children to work in pairs and list three things that they remember about the story. Read 'Bertie and the Lion' and discuss how mum helps Bertie rescue the cub and why did she do it. Read chapter 5 - 'Running Free' - Bertie goes to boarding school and is told that the cub is going to be sold to a circus. Do a conscience alley for how mum, dad and Bertie feel about the cub being sold. Share their responses. Success Criteria for Front Cover 1. It incorporates descriptions from the book 2. Eye Catching/but not too busy	Children to complete front covers in groups. MG with Guided Writing group. Resources - **copies of The Butterfly Lion**	Play Walking Bus with the class. Play music and when it stops the children have to discuss how they feel about lions in circuses. Repeat with different examples...	Children are able to create a front cover for *The Butterfly Lion.*
Thursday **Read Ch 7** **& 8**	**T1 T8** Play The 60-second challenge where a volunteer has to say what has happened in the story so far. Read chapter 7 - 'Strawbridge' and highlight the fact that the story goes forward in time. Discuss how the lady met Bertie. Read chapter 8 - 'And All's Well'. Re-read the letter on page 76 of the book and ask the children how Bertie would have felt going to war and how Millie would feel. Share their answers. Explain to the children that they are going to write a letter from Millie to Bertie or from Bertie to his Dad. Reinforce how to write a letter, the use of emotive language and relating the evidence to the book.	Children to write letters from: Millie to Bertie or from Bertie to his dad. MG with Guided Writing group. Resources - **copies of The Butterfly Lion**	Children to read out their letters to the rest of the class.	Children are able to write a letter based around the book.

Acknowledgements are due to Martin Gater for permission to reproduce this plan.

pleasure, picture books can motivate struggling or reluctant readers who are unable or unwilling to engage with other fiction texts. The dramatic effect on older non-readers of discovering or rediscovering picture books has been well documented (Martin, 1989; Smith and Alcock, 1990).

Lessons from the children

Some children in my pupil Reading Surveys lamented the progression they felt they were expected to make from picture book texts to novels, which did not have the same level of illustration.

- *I like reading but I like coloured pictures. Now I'm on a stage where I don't get coloured pictures.*
- *I like books with pictures in them, not black and white.*
- *I like books with colour and pictures.*
- *I like reading but I don't without pictures.*
- *I don't really like reading but I love picture books.*

These comments suggest how the transition is often a sudden one for young readers, and can damage reading for pleasure. To have to move from the rich artistic world of mixed media picture books, with their sophisticated visual and verbal interactions, to the comparatively bare pages of chapter books, with their dense chunks of text interrupted only by the occasional line drawing, can be daunting. It is a transition that many children feel under pressure from parents, teachers and peers to make earlier than necessary, the underlying rationale being that if you can read you don't need the pictures to help you any more. This idea of course completely misunderstands and devalues the art of the picture book and reduces it to a tool for teaching reading rather than a uniquely pleasurable form of reading open to even the youngest reader, and able to transcend boundaries of age, language, class, culture and race.

Good picture books share the same fundamental characteristics, whether for later primary or early years children.

- They can be read at different levels by readers with different experience and ability.
- They are open texts which encourage gap-filling and interpretation.
- They invite an interactive approach, since the two discourses of words and pictures have to be combined in the act of reading.
- There are discernible patterns and rhythms in the words and the pictures.
- Pictures and words are inter-dependent and inseparable: it is impossible to say which came first, or to take away one without impairing the meaning of the whole.
- There is usually humour, though for older readers this can be irony and satire.

Picture books produced specifically for older readers retain and extend the visual stimulus of early years texts, but with an increased sophistication in the written text and in the way themes and issues are handled. Books such as Raymond Briggs's *When the Wind Blows* and *The Tin-Pot Foreign General and the Old Iron Woman*, Roberto Innocenti and Ian McEwan's *Rose Blanche*, Michael Foreman's *War Game,* or Libby Hathorn and Gregory Rogers's *Way Home* offer experience of varied and sophisticated artistic styles as well as exploration of difficult issues and challenging social or political commentary.

However, because the best picture books are open to interpretation at different levels, older children can return to texts or versions of texts they first encountered at KS1 and find new interest in them. For example, picture books that provide a new visual or verbal take on traditional tales, such as Anthony Browne's *Hansel and Gretel,* Fiona French's *Snow White in New York*, Eugene Trivizas and Helen Oxenbury's *The Three Little Wolves and the Big Bad Pig,* or Jon Scieszka and Steve Johnson's *The Frog Prince Continued*, can be appealing to older readers, particularly if the books are looked at together as a group of related texts. KS2 pupils are also usually in a better position as readers to appreciate the emotional nuances of picture books dealing with family and social relationships such as Jenny Wagner and Ron Brooks's *John Brown, Rose and the Midnight Cat,* Anthony Browne's *Gorilla* and *Voices in the Park*, John Burningham's *Granpa,* or David McKee's *Not Now, Bernard.*

What David Lewis (1990) has called the 'metafictive' element in some contemporary picture books is also an aspect that older readers can more consciously enjoy. Books such as John Burningham's *Come Away from the Water, Shirley*, Anthony Browne's *Bear Hunt* or Jill Murphy's *On the Way Home* exploit their status as fictional constructs by breaking artistic boundaries, whether through characters rubbing out lines in the drawings and breaking through picture frames, or through placing different versions of reality side by side. As Lewis points out, the pleasures offered by these texts to the knowing reader are akin to those enjoyed by adult readers of the postmodern fiction of writers such as Julian Barnes, Italo Calvino, John Fowles or Umberto Eco, which also tease us by questioning the relationship between fiction and reality.

Picture book readers at KS2 also bring to the texts an increased appreciation of how language is used for effect, for example in the made-up games of Russell Hoban and Quentin Blake's *How Tom Beat Captain Najork and his Hired Sportsmen*, the extravagant sentences of John Burningham's *Would You Rather...* and *Where's Julius?*, or the alien perspective of life on earth in Jeanne Willis and Tony Ross's *Dr Xargle's Book of Earthlets*. Returning to these texts with more experienced eyes allows older readers to realise that the most effective picture books are 'not so simple' as perhaps they first appear (Baddeley and Eddershaw 1994).

As Baddeley and Eddershaw also point out (1994: 63), there is a 'precarious balance' to be preserved between 'maintaining the enjoyable experience' of picture books for older readers, and making explicit how they work in terms of language and image. Often simply making picture books available in the KS2 classroom for whole-class, group, paired or individual reading, and creating opportunities for sharing and discussing them is enough. However, there are plenty of activities which, sensitively handled, can help older readers explore the interplay of verbal and visual elements and so increase their enjoyment of picture book texts. Examples might include:

- producing alternative illustrations to accompany the text;
- writing alternative text to go with the illustrations;
- looking at the artistic techniques used;
- looking at how language is used;
- looking at the style of one picture book author across a range of titles;
- comparing the styles of two or more authors;
- pupils researching, designing and creating their own picture books.

In the case study schools mentioned below, picture books are used in KS2 classrooms in a cross-curricular approach, focusing on ways in which they can develop cognitive, affective and creative skills in older pupils. In the first school mentioned, the emphasis is on reading and enjoying picture books for their ability to develop higher order thinking skills, empathy and creative imagination in readers.

Case Study School

In this junior school, picture books such as *Rose Blanche* by Roberto Innocenti and Ian McEwan, *War Game* by Michael Foreman, *The Conquerors* by David McKee, and others, are read together in a teaching unit exploring the theme of war. As they read these picture books, the children interact with the texts through activities which ask them to provide thought or speech bubbles for characters, predict storylines, produce questions for the authors, or sketch double-page spreads to accompany written text. Drama strategies such as 'hot seating' and 'conscience alley' allow characters' motives and behaviour to be questioned, and role-play or improvisations encourage further exploration of situations and issues in the story. Other picture books give opportunities to develop thinking about gender (*Piggybook* and the *Willy the Wimp* series by Anthony Browne), race (*Amazing Grace* and *The Colour of Home* by Mary Hoffman), death (*Granpa* by John Burningham, *Badger's Parting Gifts* by Susan Varley) and social class (*Voices in the Park* by Anthony Browne). The English subject leader was inspired to use picture books with juniors in this way by a training course and has cascaded what she learnt to colleagues through staff development. She comments: 'We use picture books a lot more as a result. I think, before, a lot of the children thought picture books were quite babyish, until they really got into them, when they realised that they were actually quite deep'.

In the second school, below, picture books are read, discussed, performed, filmed and rewritten by older pupils as part of integrated creative arts work.

Case Study School

In this primary school, the English subject leader uses picture books with Year 6 pupils as part of a creative curriculum where art, drama, media and literacy work are all closely connected. She comments: 'If we look at a picture book we are looking at the art, we are looking at how the picture informs the text, we are looking at how drama can be taken from the text, even at filming it and talking about it'. A recent project involved *The Mysteries of Harris Burdick* by Chris Van Allsburg. This picture book consists of a set of 14 enigmatic illustrations each with a title and caption, which were supposedly left with a publisher by the mysterious artist, Harris Burdick, who never returned with the stories meant to accompany them. The children discussed at length each illustration and the type of story it might come from, and then produced narratives of their own to go with the pictures, using the title given and taking the caption as the first line. Their solutions to *The Mysteries of Harris Burdick* were highly imaginative and very sensitive to the elements of different story genres. The children's stories were carefully edited, published as a book with the original illustrations, using ICT, and then shared and celebrated with a wide readership within the school.

Action Point

Choose two or three picture books for older primary pupils from the Resources listed in Chapter 7. Think of a particular year group at KS2 and jot down ideas for how you would present the texts to children of this age. You could focus on aspects of content, such as any issues raised in the books, or aspects of form, such as the artistic styles used, or both.

Poetry

Even teachers who successfully nurture a love of reading in KS2 pupils through novels and picture books still sometimes struggle with poetry. As primary children get older, research shows that attitudes to poetry reading in particular become more negative (Lockwood, 1998). This is probably connected with the trend for poetry teaching to become more formal the older pupils get. There is a tendency for teachers to feel that poetry work at the end of KS2 needs to be mostly analytical and to involve much naming of the parts. This is sometimes justified as being necessary preparation for national tests or for secondary school. However, it is possibly also the result of teachers falling back on their own experiences of poetry learning, which probably involved a 'practical criticism' approach where unseen poems were dissected in order to extract their 'hidden meanings'.

In schools where KS2 children continue to enjoy poems, the active approach used with songs and rhymes at KS1 carries on. Because good poems are usually a 'fresh listen' as well as a 'fresh look', to use Robert Frost's terms, they need to be read aloud for all readers not just younger ones. James Carter points out that many contemporary children's poets such as himself make their livings as performers, and so write for the stage as well as the page (Carter, 2007: 15), but most older poems also benefit from being heard as well as seen, as with the Hilaire Belloc poems in the plans below. Going further and encouraging children to perform and present poems using drama techniques allows them to get inside poems and explore them actively and collaboratively. Regular poetry performances for a variety of audiences help spread the word that poetry is for enjoyment by performers as well as audience.

The plan shown in Table 4.2, produced to fit the requirements of the original NLS framework, is an extract only and represents the second week of a two-week poetry unit taught to Year 6 children. The week begins with shared reading aloud and paired oral discussion of a classic Hilaire Belloc poem, before moving on to group activities involving drama and expressive reading. As the week progresses, the children continue to hear the poem and other Belloc poems read aloud, give their personal responses to the poem in words or drawings, use the Internet to find out more about the poet and his poems, and then move through prose writing and drafts towards creating their own cautionary tale like Belloc's. The whole week shows the teacher's high expectations of what older primary children can achieve in terms of reading, writing, speaking and listening to poems, and above all enjoying them.

There also needs to be time for individual reading of poems on the page and the right environment for this. Children need the opportunity to browse through a variety of poetry books in a comfortable and relaxed setting. The rights of the reader of poetry books, to adapt Daniel Pennac's charter (Pennac, 2006) include the right not to read from beginning to end but to dip in, the right to read and re-read favourite poems, the right to read them aloud, the right to learn them by heart, the right to read anything you consider poetry, and the right not to finish a poetry book if you don't like it.

Poems can be taken apart from time to time, like any well-made objects, but it is important to remember to put them back together again properly at the end and check that they still work. Looking at how a poet has built up sound patterns through rhythm, rhyme, alliteration, assonance, onomatopoeia and other devices, or how word pictures have been built up through images, or meanings made through puns and word play, can add a different sort of enjoyment as well as understanding of poems. But poems should not be used just as excuses for feature-spotting, for example hunting down metaphors and similes for the sake of a naming of the parts. Poems are often left in pieces after this kind of activity as the lesson moves on to ransacking another text for the same feature or topic. It should be a rule to read the poem aloud again after any form of analysis, relishing its sounds and images anew after the insight into how they fit together.

Table 4.2 *Extract from the short-term planning for a unit on poetry with 10–11-year-olds*

Day	Shared text and sentence Level	Guided reading and writing	Independent work: 5 groups differentiated into AA/A/BA levels	ICT/ Cross-curricular links	Resources	Plenary
Mon	Read 'Jim, who ran away from his nurse and was eaten by a lion' by Hilaire Belloc Shared reading; paired discussion – reader response Explore the very obvious rhythm; archaic words; etc.	Work with a group to improve interpretations Teacher (T.) with group 5, Teaching Assistant (T.A.) with group 4	Group1: pupils learn stanza 1 ready for recitation in the plenary. Drama: the group prepares mime and movement for stanza Groups 2–4: in their groups, pupils learn stanzas 2, 3, 4 respectively ready for recitation in the plenary Group 5: pupils prepare an expressive reading of stanza 5 from the poem. As this is the finale, good expression and intonation are essential	Drama	Copies of the poem Coloured pens to annotate poem Tape recorder and tape for T.A. to use in plenary	Group 1 leads by performing their mime Touch thoughts Class performs the poem as much as possible from memory T.A. tapes the rendition! What is the effect of intonation? Understanding of the poem at the end of the lesson?
Tue	Re-read the poem Deepen exploration of voice, theme and particularly form – rhyme scheme, vocabulary choice, the outrageous with the	Support a group in their drawing T. with group 4, T.A. with group 5	Groups 1 and 2: write about their response to the poem. Include authorial intention, and whether they agree with moralising in poetry as a tool in parenting!	Art History: Victorians (in year 5)	Copies of the poem Coloured pens to annotate poem	Group 4 leads: share some of the sketches Feed in the authorial intention and pupils' views of

	prosaic, comedic with cautionary tale, overall effect; authorial intention		Group 3: write their response to the poem. Do you agree with Belloc's approach in telling a moral tale in poetry? Explore Groups 4 and 5: Give pairs a stanza to represent by drawing quick sketches Write a short response to the poem if time allows Group 1 on computer – word process their ideas	OHT and OHT pens Scaffold sheets: groups 1, 2, 3	the tale from groups 1 and 2 Do the rest of the class feel sketches represent the poem? Draw some conclusions about the poem/poet as a result of exploring this example Look forward to tomorrow – considering another poem by this poet Using smart board go to www.theotherpages.org/poems/belloc. Ask pupils to explore for homework
Wed	Read 'Tarantella' by Belloc Reader response. 'But what I am not sure of' activity. What questions would you want to ask the voice in the poem? Read again; particularly explore sound, rhythm	Support a group in their writing. T. with group 3, T.A. with group 5	Groups 1 and 2: pupils rework the poem in a different form: write the narrative poem as a letter to Miranda Groups 3 and 4: find rhyme scheme by annotating poem; identify refrain. Can they begin to suggest why refrain used and the effect?	History Copies of the poem Coloured pens to annotate poem	Group 3 lead: give ideas on rhyme scheme and refrain. Can they begin to suggest why refrain used and the effect? Ask pupils to compare this poem with 'Jim' Comments?

(Continued)

Table 4.2 (Continued)

Day	Whole class/shared work	Teacher/T.A. roles	Group work	History	Resources	Plenary (Similarities? Differences?)
			Group 5: find rhyme scheme by annotating poem; identify refrain. If time, highlight any words they are not sure of, and discuss with T.A. Group 5 on computer: use colours to highlight findings			Similarities? Differences?
Thu	Read 'Rebecca, who slammed doors for fun and perished miserably' by Belloc. Shared reading; paired discussion – reader response. Explore language, theme, form. Gather together ideas about characteristics of Belloc's poetry studied so far. Make a checklist on the board (Lead towards cautionary tale if it doesn't come up immediately)	Support pupils in their writing. T. with group 2, T.A. with group 1	All groups: pupils discuss in pairs ideas for writing their own cautionary tale poem inspired by the poet; pupils then write the 'story' or narrative of their chosen idea in prose; make jottings of ideas for the odd line in poetic form. Group 2 on computer to jot down ideas	History	Copies of the poem. Coloured pens to annotate. poem checklist	Group 2 lead: share some results. Praise cautionary tales. Pupils give others tips on how to improve these first attempts
Fri	Shared writing: T. negotiates beforehand with a pupil to use their work as the focus of the shared writing (trust). T. shows copy of narrative on the board	Support pupils in their writing. T. with group 1, T.A. with group 5	Pupils write a first draft of their poem, using the teaching tips given in the shared/guided writing session (30 mins). Group 3 on computer to write first draft		Pupil's work	Group 5 lead: pupils share their work with response partner. Group 1 share their poems with the class. Comments and supportive criticism

	T. with help of pupils writes draft of poem Redraft, guiding and voicing ideas and views as composition unfolds (15 mins to allow time for composing)				T. overview: bring together the strands of this unit, hold discussion to compare and contrast poet's work; underline key teaching objectives at text, sentence and word level Discuss: Have we met the objectives of this unit? (15 mins)
Extended writing	Set up session – what we need to do to be ready to write etc. Recall this morning's discussions.	T. works with 3 groups (1, 3, 5), supporting and guiding to improve on first drafts TA with groups 4, 2	Pupils redraft their poems using teaching tips, checklist and ideas from the plenary Group 4 on computer to write first draft	Checklist	Pupils share their work with response partner Groups share their poems with the class Comments and supportive criticism T. overview: take work in for detailed marking

Acknowledgement is due to Carolyn Ripper for permission to reproduce this plan.

Ways of Promoting Reading for Pleasure

Other examples of successful practice in promoting the enjoyment of reading at KS2 can be summarised under the same six headings used in the previous chapter, though again there will be some overlap between them.

Activities that are open and authentic

- **Using creative activities as responses to books read, featuring music, dance, drama, art, sculpture, ICT, design and technology (DT) or combinations of these.** For example, art and DT could be combined in designing and making life-size models of book characters that express children's reactions to the characters concerned. Music, ICT and dance could be used to create appropriate sound and movement to accompany the performance of a poem, which could be recorded onto video or DVD, along the lines of a music video.
- **Children making their own personal anthology of poems.** Creating a personal poetry anthology, in a format that is continually expandable, is a way in which children can take ownership of poetry and be aware of their own development as readers. Poems can be written or typed out in appropriate fonts and styles and accompanied by illustrations. Children's own anthologies can be shelved with published ones to build or expand a poetry library.
- **Organising regular author visits and arranging for groups of children to read different books by the author and prepare questions to ask.** Pupils can discuss what they think the author will be like, and why he or she writes about particular themes, events or issues, based on books read beforehand. They can then interview the author during the visit and discover how accurate their preconceptions were.
- **Shadowing the process of appointing the new Children's Laureate every two years.** Children can use the Laureate website to research previous holders of the post and find information about the activities of the current one (www.childrenslaureate.org.uk). They can draw up their own shortlist of nominations for the next Laureateship and set up an appointments committee to consider who is the best candidate and why, hearing submissions from different groups about the authors they are backing. Near to the time of the Laureate's appointment, children can send in their individual and group nominations to the website.
- **Devising a school or class version of national television book programmes such as *The Big Read, Battle of the Books*, or *The Big Bad Read*, where participants have to argue for the merits of particular books or characters.** Children can produce leaflets and posters promoting the books they are supporting and give presentations in assemblies to encourage others to vote for their choices. The final shortlist of competing books can be displayed in the school library along with publicity material from publishers and local bookshops.

- **Researching authors and presenting the findings as pages on the school website.** This will work best, of course, where the authors are ones who have visited or will be visiting the school, or where the children are focusing on the particular writers' books. All publishers and most well-known authors now have their own websites, with specific pages aimed at children. There are also many other child-friendly websites with information about authors and books, as well as accessible printed guides to children's literature (see Resources in Chapter 7). Children will need guidance and support to ensure that researching and presenting electronic material does not become just a cutting and pasting exercise.

- **Getting children to order new library books and review them when they arrive.** Buying, opening and reading a brand new book, especially a hardback with its own particular smell and feel, is one of the pleasures that children should experience if we want to get them hooked on reading. Many children from less advantaged backgrounds may not experience this in the later primary years unless it is through school. Rather than being too possessive about new school or classroom library books, we need to let the children feel a sense of ownership of them individually and collectively. Involving them in the whole process of acquiring, recommending and distributing new library stock nurtures respect for and appreciation of books.

- **Making regular links between reading and writing activities, not only in relation to books read but also to popular forms of children's leisure reading such as song lyrics, football fanzines, personal interest magazines, websites and blogs.** Reading and writing are mutually reinforcing activities that feed off each other, most of all when they are linked to children's real interests. However, when writing tasks related to reading are artificial or merely routine, as book reviewing often is, the effect on engagement with reading is usually negative. Giving children opportunities to write in and about a wide variety of popular cultural forms that reflect their own pleasure reading habits increases motivation and can lead to improved attitudes to reading across the board, as well as improvements in writing.

- **Having a non-recording day or session each week, where the emphasis is on interacting with texts through oral activities rather than written outcomes.** Although writing can stimulate enjoyment of reading, as above, there are times when it is good to remove the expectation that writing will always follow reading activities, either as an assessment or to record outcomes from it. Arranging for some periods where children are able to engage in a variety of reading activities without the pressure of written outcomes can help nurture reading enjoyment. Children also come to see oral responses to texts, such as freeze frames, spoken presentations or group discussions, as legitimate ways of expressing reactions to what they have read.

A reading environment where there is easy access to plenty of suitable texts

- **Ensuring that the range of classroom reading material is wide and up-to-date; including, for example, graphic novels, *manga* books, newspapers, comics, special interest magazines and electronic texts as well as books.** This is an opportunity to extend children's reading enjoyment as well as provide what they already know and like. Comics, newspapers and magazines, for example, can be ones that children would not necessarily encounter at home. A balanced reading diet needs to be promoted also, so that children are encouraged to try different things and not to feel there is only one type of reading they like.

- **Including CDs or cassette tapes of appropriate books in the classroom library, alongside the books themselves.** Well-read audio books are a half-way house between storytelling and reading. They provide a powerful listening experience, but also allow individual rewinding and reviewing, as reading does. Many children experience the pleasures of listening to audio books from an early age as part of car journeys or bedtime routines. Children can use them in the classroom as a way of enjoying books they might not otherwise be able to manage on their own or as an enhancement of the reading experience for more manageable or familiar texts.

- **Including fiction, drama and non-fiction texts written by children, and audio books narrated by them, in the classroom library.** This provides the ultimate link between children's reading and writing, when they are able to enjoy reading each other's work or listening to readings recorded by other pupils. The use of sophisticated ICT software for creating written and spoken word texts has made this a much more realistic option for primary schools.

- **Ensuring that the school library contains up-to-date books from or about other countries and cultures, including translated fiction.** In the United Kingdom only about 2% of children's books were originally published in a language other than the mother tongue compared with something like 40% in continental Europe. Readers tend to forget that familiar classics such as the *Moomin* books or the *Pippi Longstocking* series are translations. Contemporary European fiction like Daniel Pennac's *The Eye of the Wolf* (Walker, 2002) or Reinhardt Jung's *Bambert's Book of Missing Stories* (Egmont, 2002) can give children different reading pleasures as well as insights into other worlds. There are excellent guides available to translated children's books and ordering is very easy using Internet booksellers (see Resources in Chapter 7). There is also now a prize for the best-translated children's book each year, the Marsh Award for Children's Literature in Translation. As an incentive to read widely in geographic terms, children can be given a Reading Passport which they 'stamp' with details of books they have read from different parts of the world.

Pupil choice

- **Displaying children's selections of books in the school library and classrooms, using the model of bookshop 'staff picks'.** There has been a revolution in recent years in how bookshops, and to a lesser extent public libraries, display books. Far more books are now 'front on' rather than 'spine on', and there is much more emphasis on displaying reader advice and recommendations in the form of posters and cards. There is no reason why schools should not follow this example and involve children in the choosing and recommending process as much as possible. Local bookshops and libraries are often happy to give expert advice and help in this area, if only as a way of developing potential customers of the future.

- **Involving older children in making story sacks for younger readers in the nursery or KS1.** Story sacks, in which relevant artefacts, games, audio books, puppets or soft toys are packaged together with a copy of a storybook, have been used widely to enhance reading enjoyment, particularly for adults sharing books with younger readers. However, choosing the contents of the sacks themselves is a valuable activity for older pupils, enabling them to use their knowledge of books imaginatively to try to capture younger readers' interest. Older readers making story sacks linked to novels read by their peers (maybe rechristened 'book packs' or something similar) is also very worthwhile both for readers and pack-makers.

- **Asking children to compile lists of, for example, '12 books to read before you're 12' and so on.** 'List-mania' is as rife among children as adults. There are many other ways of tapping into this list-making compulsion that can be used to promote reading, for example 'top ten heroes', 'top five baddies', or a termly 'reading top twenty'.

- **Inviting children to help with a classroom or school library 'weeding out' day,** when outdated or outworn books are removed from the shelves and sent for re-use or recycling. Children are well placed to suggest which fiction and non-fiction books are past their 'use by' date, either because of their condition or their content, and need to make way for something newer. They may even be able to find homes for some of the volumes 'retired' on the grounds of poor condition.

- **Inviting children to donate or lend new books to the classroom library.** Children can also help in refilling the gaps on classroom bookshelves after a stock-taking activity such as the above, either by suggesting new acquisitions or, if they are willing and able, lending or giving copies of their own favourites (although nothing that is too special).

- **Using children as 'focus groups' to test out new ideas for reading development in school.** Again, pupils are best placed to give a consumer view of proposals to revamp the library, introduce incentive schemes for reading, arrange a programme for a book event, or similar. Using a 'Reading Suggestions Box' in the library gives an opportunity for pupils to offer ideas for reading promotion. Ideas that are adopted can then receive an appropriate reward.

Collaborative learning

- **Ensuring that there are opportunities for group activities where children can read and talk about shared texts together, in addition to teacher-directed guided reading groups.** These can be one-off activities using texts such as playscripts, for example. Texts such as these, where there are opportunities for all children to take part, are ideal for sharing in independent group work. But pupil-directed groups can also meet regularly as reading circles to discuss responses to shared class texts or to individual reading, taking as their starting point comments recorded in pupils' reading or response journals.

- **Setting up reading links with local secondary schools.** This can involve two-way traffic. Secondary pupils and their teachers can visit feeder primaries for regular contact, such as reading buddy schemes, and also for one-off events, such as book weeks or shadowing book awards. Equally, older primary pupils and their teachers can visit secondary schools for reading quizzes, poetry presentations or storytelling sessions.

- **Posting pupils' reading recommendations and reviews on the school intranet for other children to access.** Having a section of the school website where children and teachers can contribute regular comments about pleasure reading of all kinds, both school-related and home-based, is an effective way of raising the profile of reading for enjoyment using ICT. Contributors can add their own 'Reader Review' and star rating for books featured, using the model of Internet bookstores' 'Customer Reviews'. Including reading suggestions, along the lines of 'If you enjoyed this book, you might also enjoy … ', makes a useful resource that pupils can search or browse through for suggestions about what to read next.

- **Having a Reading Wall where pupils and staff can post reading-related items and news.** This is essentially a physical version of an intranet webpage, which has a more immediate and visible impact on the school reading environment. The concept of a 'wall' to which handwritten items can easily be fixed appeals to children, and is more informal, easier to monitor and keep up to date. If children get into the habit of checking the wall regularly, it can be used for announcements about book events, library news, book quizzes and so forth.

- **Encouraging older children to become 'reading coaches' or motivators who devise ways of promoting reading with their peers.** This could be organised as part of the National Literacy Trust's *Reading Champions* scheme mentioned in Chapter 5, or as a programme of the school's own devising. Pupils themselves are usually in the best position to advise on what kind of reading promotion will work with their peers. The idea of being a kind of 'Personal Reading Trainer' to other pupils and devising individual 'Reading Fitness Programmes' for them can appeal to keen readers who are confident and influential with their peers. The sporting analogy also helps motivate those who are being coached.

- **Encouraging children, including less able readers, to record reviews of books on tape, as part of a book programme for other pupils to listen to.** For some children, particularly those who are not fluent writers, recording their comments about books and reading on tape, or as an audio file on a computer, is liberating. These oral reviews can be edited to make a kind of radio book programme for other pupils to listen to via headphones as part of library sessions or in silent reading time. Features about favourite authors, interviews with adults about their favourite children's books, and group readings of poems and extracts can be added too.
- **'Interviewing' an author in groups by devising questions and using role-play and 'hot seating'.** Using minimal props, such as pretend microphones, children can work in groups to role-play interviews with children's writers. The authors should be those whose books the children have recently read, and research will need to be done beforehand to inform the questions and answers the children will have to devise. One child can be hot-seated as the author to field questions from the interviewer(s), or the children can take it in turns to be in the hot seat. The interviews could be 'performed' for other groups to watch, with further questions to the author being invited from the audience via a roving 'microphone'.

An approach where pupils are aware of what they are doing and how and why they are doing it

- **Using Reader Journals to enable older children not only to log what they read, but also to reflect on how and why they read.** These differ from reading journals as they are commonly used because they provide opportunities for older pupils to think about themselves as readers, rather than simply recording the details of books they have read. In a Reader Journal, children begin by sketching a brief reading autobiography, family tree, or timeline, where they look back on their own personal history as readers and maybe that of other family members. They then go on to take a broader view of themselves as readers and reflect on the pattern of their reading, their tastes and preferences, how these developed over time, and how they see themselves developing in the future. They can reflect on why they read what they do, how they like to read, where they like reading and what they get out of reading. The Journal can also include information and pictures relating to themselves and family members as readers, as well as to favourite books, authors or films of books, and can include extracts from favourite texts.
- **Encouraging pupils to contribute comments, milestones or targets to their own reading records.** The Reader Journal can feed into teachers' own formative record-keeping. Pupils can add short profiles of how they see themselves as readers and record significant achievements they feel they have made. Reading targets set by teachers are a fact of life for primary school readers, but are likely to be more useful if pupils have a hand in drawing them up, monitoring them and assessing when they have been met.

- **Getting groups of pupils to carry out surveys of favourite books in different year groups to inform school book purchases.** The children can research their recommended book purchases on publishers' websites or Internet bookshops. They can then make PowerPoint presentations of their survey findings and purchasing recommendations in assemblies or at School Council meetings.
- **Planning a media advertising campaign to promote a National Year of Reading.** Children can be challenged to produce posters, bookmarks, competitions and magazine, radio or TV adverts to publicise a national reading campaign aimed at families. A good slogan and logo would be needed to focus the campaign. The project could tie in with developing persuasive writing and with work to develop critical reading of media texts.
- **Designing consumer advice to go on the back covers of children's books, along the lines of information given about food, to inform a healthy reading diet.** Children's books now sometimes come with warnings about content and suitability for certain age-ranges, so this idea continues that trend. What constitutes 'healthy reading' is obviously debatable, so the emphasis would be on informing the 'consumer' of the book about what 'ingredients' it contained, what genre it belonged to, who might enjoy it and maybe some 'serving suggestions' in terms of how, when and where it would be best to enjoy the book. This could be in the form of a label to stick on the back cover of the book, a bookmark, or an information card.

Links between reading inside and outside the classroom

The aim here is to show children how readers in the world beyond the school read for pleasure as well as for a variety of other purposes in their daily lives.

- **Arranging for older children to survey reading habits in the local community, for example by interviewing library users or bookshop customers.** This project would fit in well with cross-curricular work involving preparing interview questions and data handling. Local bookshops are usually happy to accommodate pupil interviewers outside of peak shopping times, and staff as well as customers are often very forthcoming about their book choices and buying habits. Libraries are also usually willing to provide access for children to interview their visitors, or alternatively to circulate written questionnaires that children have devised. Findings can be presented using ICT and copies sent to the participating bookshop or library for display.
- **Arranging for children to interview their family members about what they read when young and what they read now.** Children can be encouraged to approach readers of different ages, grandparents, aunts and uncles, as well as parents and siblings, with a set of agreed interview questions about childhood reading. Results can be shared with other children in groups and compared with the children's own present day reading preferences. As a whole class, children can consider generational differences and

any enduring patterns in childhood reading over time. Are there any books which were favourites for all the age groups interviewed? This project has the useful side effect of promoting conversations about reading in homes where they might not otherwise take place.

- **Inviting members of local book groups to come to school to speak to each class about why they enjoy reading and discussing books.** Adult reading groups are a leisure interest of recent times that has grown dramatically in popularity. Children are often unaware of how widespread these groups are in most local communities. Members are usually delighted to be invited to school to talk about what they read and how they organise their meetings. Sometimes the reading group can be persuaded to read a contemporary children's book and the members can then discuss this with groups of children who have also read it in a simulation of a reading group meeting.

- **Writing letters to celebrities about their favourite books and making a display from replies received.** This is clearly an activity that will depend on the goodwill of those to whom the children choose to write, if it is to succeed. However, teachers can make suggestions for likely candidates by looking on websites such as the National Literacy Trust's to research those sporting and other celebrities who have been involved in *Reading Champions* and other campaigns, and so have already declared an interest in promoting reading with young people.

- **Looking at biographies, autobiographies and websites about authors to find out how reading has been important in their lives.** Most author websites contain interviews or articles where the writers mention books that have been important for them, particularly when they were young. Children can use this information to make a display of authors and their favourite childhood reads. They can also devise quizzes where authors have to be matched up with photographs of themselves when young and the titles of the children's books they remember best.

Pause for Thought

Think of one further strategy for promoting positive engagement with reading to include under each of the six headings above.

Chapter **5**

Getting Boys Reading for Pleasure

Summary

Chapter 5 considers the 'gender gap' in reading for pleasure in UK primary schools and reviews recent government initiatives aimed at addressing it. Strategies used in schools that have successfully engaged boys' interest in books and reading are then discussed and illustrated by case study examples, particularly the use of reading journals, literature circles and interactive whiteboards. The importance of providing reading role models for boys is emphasised and examples of good practice highlighted.

The Gender Gap

The gender gap in attainment in English at KS1 and KS2 is well known, though in the figures for the 2007 Standard Assessment Tests (SATs) the gap between girls and boys is wider in writing, especially for the older pupils (11% at level 2+ and 15% at level 4+), than in reading (8% and 6%, respectively). The gap between boys' and girls' reading attainment is not a phenomenon confined to the United Kingdom, as the PIRLS and PISA surveys make clear, but the gap in English schools is particularly marked. Internationally, England ranked 27th out of 35 countries in difference in the achievement of boys and girls in the 2001 PIRLS survey, and the difference between the scores of boys and girls when reading for literary purposes, as opposed to information purposes, was particularly high (Twist et al., 2003: 24–25, 28).

The schools inspectorate Ofsted's survey *English 2000–05: A Review of Inspection Evidence* (2005) also identified boys right across the primary age-range as causing particular concern with respect to attitudes to reading, wider reading and reading for pleasure: 'Boys tend to give up independent reading more easily than girls and, as they get older, seem to have greater difficulty in finding books to enjoy' (p. 32). In my own survey of 1400 pupils in schools where reading for enjoyment was successfully promoted, I still found a significant gender gap. For example, in response to a prompt such as 'Reading a book is something I like to do', 77% of boys said 'often' compared with over 91% of girls, and 7% of boys said 'never' compared with just over 1% of girls.

It has been claimed that 'sex is the major factor in studies of children as readers, being more strongly linked than either social class or ability and attainment with how much children read' (Barrs and Pidgeon, 1993: 1). Not only are there differences in how well boys read, what they read and how much they read, but also in how they discuss their reading and how they perform in particular kinds of assessments of reading. Researchers in this field have also identified particular aspects of English as a subject which tend to alienate boys. The emphasis on reading narrative fiction, and usually realist fiction dealing with everyday interpersonal relationships, puts boys at a disadvantage. Boys' reading interests outside school, particularly as they get older, tend to be more in fantasy fiction than realism, and more in non-fiction genres than those of girls. My own research recorded significantly more boys enjoying non-fiction than girls, 72% as opposed to only 57% of girls.

In addition, English subject teachers' preference for personal responses to fiction reading doubly disadvantages boys because of their notorious reluctance to display emotional involvement with their reading in public. This can lead to what Elaine Millard has called 'a dissonance between the literacy they [boys] practised skilfully at home and that demanded from them by teachers', since 'evidence suggests that there is less provision for boys to exercise their reading interests within the school environment than those that are seen as appropriate for girls' (Millard, 1997: 13).

The lack of a male reading role model either at home or at school is clearly a serious problem for many boys. The National Literacy Trust reading survey of over 8000 pupils aged 4–18 in 2005 found that 25% never saw their father read (www.literacytrust.org.uk). There is a danger that reading, especially leisure reading, is seen by boys not as a neutral activity but as a gender-specific one, associated with women and girls. In my survey of over 300 primary school parents, I discovered that their children were ten times more likely to read and talk about books with their mother than with their father. There is evidence also that representations of reading in English-speaking countries, for example on greetings cards and on children's book covers, tend to portray it as a feminine activity (Millard, 1997: 19–20).

The role models that boys find in children's stories, should they read them, also seem to have changed over time so that 'uncomplicated, unreflective, anti-intellectual and non-reading males became the fictional role models for a generation of boys' (Reynolds in Bleach 1998: 6–7). Paradoxically, a publishing house, Elliott and Thompson, recently founded to provide books just for men and boys, promises to present a diet of just such hero figures, according to the newspaper article reporting on it, headlined 'Forget the namby-pamby girly stuff, here are ripping yarns for real chaps':

> Problems with boys reading less and later than girls, teenage male crime and the rising male suicide rate, were clear signs that boys needed stronger role models, said Mr Elliott. 'I think we need more books demonstrating what I would call masculine principles and masculine emotions.' (*Daily Telegraph*, 2003: 3)

Concern about a widening gender gap in British schools has also prompted direct government intervention. The UK government set up a scheme in 2007 called 'Boys into Books' as part of its efforts to close the 'reading gap' between boys and girls. As noted, this scheme promised to 'put a boys' bookshelf in every secondary school library in the country containing positive, modern, relevant role models for boys' in order to encourage boys' reading (www.standards.dfes. gov.uk). An official booklist was published shortly afterwards by the School Library Association, containing a mix of classic and contemporary fiction genres such as spy, thriller, science fiction and adventure stories, along with non-fiction, and secondary school libraries were able to select 20 free books from it to stock their boys' bookshelf (www.sla.org.uk). In launching the scheme, the Education Secretary acknowledged the importance of reading for enjoyment:

> We know there is a clear link between reading for pleasure and academic performance – not just in English, but across the whole curriculum. Beyond this, of course, reading can enrich their (children's) lives by freeing their imagination, inspiring creativity and developing intellectual curiosity. Boys tend to read less than girls, and some lose the reading bug completely after they change schools at 11. This initiative will help boys re-acquire the reading habit, and try out a wider range of great books. (www.dfes.gov.uk)

Pause for Thought

Can the 'gender gap' in reading ever be closed? Would initiatives aimed at encouraging boys to read for pleasure have a corresponding positive effect on girls' reading habits too, thus preserving the gap? Would it be right to exclude girls from opportunities to develop enjoyment in reading if they were offered to boys only? Does the 'gender gap' matter, as long as the majority of boys and girls are positive about reading and there is an upward trend in the reading attitudes of both?

Successful Schools

In schools where reading for pleasure is an established part of the school culture and teachers are enthusiastic about books, as described in earlier chapters, this tends to be infectious for boys as well as girls. Many of these teachers report that they do not target boys with specific techniques but use the same approaches and extend the same opportunities to both sexes. For example, the subject leader at one successful school does not feed boys simply with texts specifically aimed at them, such as football-related books. Football books have a place on the class bookshelf like everything else, but she aims to widen the genres read by boys and to encourage girls to read football books too. There is a wide range of books available for a wide range of readers of both sexes. For this teacher, it is a question of being aware of what is available, getting to know what actually interests individual boys, talking to them about their home reading and reflecting this in book ordering. She finds, for example, that boys enjoy books with male heroes, with word play, visual gags and so on. Older boys also like more substantial texts such as Cornelia Funke's *The Thief Lord*, Terry Pratchett's *The Carpet People*, the *Chronicles of Ancient Darkness* series by Michelle Paver and *The Edge Chronicles* series by Paul Stewart and Chris Riddell, Philip Reeve's *Mortal Engines* books, but also picture books such as *Two Frogs* by Chris Wormell.

However, successful schools also report that some of the approaches they use for promoting reading for pleasure do work particularly well for boys. Using books on CD and audio tape proves to be an effective way of getting boys in particular hooked on fiction. For example, using the unabridged readings of the *Harry Potter* books with reluctant readers was particularly successful with boys in one school. The boys followed the printed texts as they listened to the CDs and in this way worked their way through some lengthy books, with resultant gains in attainment as well as attitude and self-image. As their teacher commented: 'They've really come on. They feel they're really making progress and always they're keen to show me what page they are up to'. As a result, the teacher expanded this initiative to make more books on CD available in the school library. Another teacher played audio tapes of stories such as Francesca Simon's *Horrid Henry* at lunchtime, when younger children were eating in the classroom, and found that this proved especially popular with boys. Boys making their own recordings of shorter fiction books on tape or CD has also been used as an effective motivator for reluctant readers (Barrs and Pidgeon, 1993: 127–128). This is an extension of the traditional fiction and non-fiction book-making activities which teachers have used for a long time to involve children of all ages in the world of printed books.

In successful schools, playscripts are regularly used as motivating reading material for children of all ages and both sexes, in whole class and group settings. The evidence suggests that these texts again appeal particularly to boys' liking for oral language alongside written. These are texts that obviously cry out for performance, whether in the form of recording on video and audio tape or classroom drama activities, and this clearly has boy-appeal. Performing play texts puts reading into a collaborative, social context that is more supportive for reluctant or unconfident readers than the normal individual engagement with literary texts, which can be unmotivating.

The reading of any literary text can be made more appealing to all pupils, but especially boys, by an active approach that includes drama techniques such as role-play or simulation, as illustrated in the previous chapters. For example, a text like Anne Fine's *Flour Babies*, about a class who have to look after sacks of flour as if they were babies, for a secondary school science project, lends itself to a real-life simulation where children are given exactly the same task. For boy readers of this novel this is a particularly challenging and engaging activity which foregrounds gender and can lead to lively debate about the roles of boys and girls more generally. One Year 6 teacher carried out this project with her class, getting them to keep diaries of their flour-baby minding, as in the book, and starting each literacy session on the book with readings from the pupils' real diaries which were compared with the fictional ones in the story. She commented at the end of the project that 'the boys were always fully involved. The project has brought the book alive for them and shown that it's fun'. Diana Sparkes has given an account elsewhere of a similar project with older pupils in an all boys' school (Barrs and Pidgeon, 1998: 38–40).

For another subject leader in a successful school, it is the approach of never rejecting any reading pupils do – whether at home or at school – which is particularly effective with boys. Recognising non-fiction, non-literary and non-print texts that boys (and girls) read for enjoyment as legitimate reading material is vitally important. This means placing such material in the school and classroom libraries, and maybe giving boys some responsibilities for ordering, cataloguing and organising it. As Hilary Minns has said: 'It is surely now time to validate this reading, so that boys can identify themselves as competent readers of a variety of texts' (in Barrs and Pidgeon, 1993: 71). In this school, children can bring in magazines and other non-fiction material from home for pleasure reading, and these are used successfully, along with electronic texts, in silent reading. Children are also encouraged to read at home every night, not necessarily to parents, and reading on a website, for example, is quite acceptable to have signed off on a child's reading record as reading at home for that evening, something which has proved popular with reluctant boys. The only requirement is that children read a mix of texts and not just one type. As the Education Secretary said in launching the National Year of Reading for 2008: 'Books, magazines, comics – the reading matter is less important than children learning to love reading. This is about far more than a book at bedtime – we want to make reading an integral part of everyone's lives' (www.standards.dfes.gov.uk).

Lessons from the children

The comments from some of the boys in my Reading Survey confirmed the need to accommodate a range of reading materials in the classroom which reflect children's home reading preferences and tastes.

- *I like reading at home but not very much at school because some of the books are boring and I want harder books.*
- *I only like Captain Underpants books.*
- *I like blood and guts books.*
- *I start to feel sleepy when I read. I'd rather read comics, funny books and newspapers, also magazines.*
- *I like comics and drawn books the best.*
- *Reading a book is boring. Reading a comic is fun.*
- *I don't like reading, only reading the papers and a magazine. I am good at it but don't like it.*

Not only did some of the boys feel that their home reading was often not recognised in school, but also sometimes that they could not talk about it there.

- *I like comics and Simpsons books. That's all I like, not any other books except Goosebumps. I never talk about it because they never let me.*

It is difficult to see boys such as these widening their reading to 'other books' in a positive way if they are not allowed to share the reading interests they currently have.

Pause for Thought

Which of the children's comments or drawings about reading in this and the previous chapters do you find most revealing and why? How would you respond to the points the children make?

Some schools take the approach of meeting gender issues in reading head on by encouraging debate that challenges stereotypes. A text such as Anne Fine's *Bill's New Frock*, where the main character becomes a girl for a day and experiences among other things the different kind of reading material offered to girls and boys at school, offers plenty of scope for animated discussion with Year 3 or 4 children. Other activities can lead to passionate debate about gendered reading material, such as asking older KS2 children to sort through books, looking at covers, blurb, first pages and author notes, and decide whether they are aimed mainly at girls, boys or both, and what features suggest this. Boys can then be asked to read the 'girls' books' and vice versa. At the resultant reporting-back session, the boy and girl readers can discuss whether their prejudices were confirmed or not.

In other successful schools, where boys' achievements in reading have given rise to particular concern, they are sometimes targeted for specific measures. These can be designed to improve boys' engagement with books and reading at classroom level, as in the first case study example below.

Case Study School

This Year 6 subject leader targeted boys strongly in her own teaching, partly through having a teaching group in which boys outnumbered girls by 5 to 1. She picked very specific books for shared reading which she knew would be exciting, 'boy-biased' and 'very strong male books'. She planned her Literacy Hour teaching around books such as *Stormbreaker* by Anthony Horowitz, David Almond's *Skellig* and *Kit's Wilderness*, and books and stories by writers like Paul Jennings and Robert Swindells. She used many drama strategies, such as hot seating, during the Literacy Hour and also got pupils to do author searches on the Internet, which boys in particular enjoyed. She also included creative activities that involved making things, such as constructing a Dr Who-style Tardis 'time machine' in the classroom during a project on science fiction books, which the boys were very excited by. The attitudes of boys to reading were much more positive after these activities, to the extent that a boys' book recommendation board, complete with pictures of the books suggested, was set up in the school's new library, and this informed stock purchases.

Initiatives can also be aimed at the whole school level, as in the second example below, from the DfES website. In both cases, though, the measures are ones that do not harm girls' attainment in and attitudes to reading.

Case Study School

Because of concern about a wide gender gap in the KS2 reading SATs, this junior school set itself the task of getting boys to enjoy fiction as well as non-fiction, to be more reflective readers, and to understand the importance of reading in the workplace. A further aim was to involve parents more in boys' reading. The initiative had the backing of the school governors, the senior management, all teachers and teaching assistants, and parents.

To begin with, parents of boys completed a reading interview form with their sons. These were designed to raise awareness of reading at home and to help guide teachers in advising pupils on their reading choices. With this information, a 'Boyzone' was created in the school, where new books that catered for boys' reported interests were made available and promoted through eye-catching displays in classrooms and the library. A 'reading bag check' was also carried out each day, in a light-hearted way, to make sure that books were taken home for reading!

Twice-weekly reading sessions were introduced, 'Magazine Monday' and 'Fiction Friday'. These were intended to benefit both boys and girls. These sessions involved group and individual reading and discussion with the teacher, but also time for boy–girl pairings of pupils to discuss each other's reading either of fiction or magazines. Boys and girls swapped books and magazines, and tried to work out what made them appeal to male or female readers. Two files, 'Girl Power' and 'Boys' Best Bets', were set up to which pupils could contribute reviews on a voluntary basis.

Finally, fathers of both boys and girls were invited to school to give talks in assembly about the reading that they did in the workplace each day as part of their job. Other assemblies featured Year 6 boys modelling how to write reflective comments about their reading in journal form.

The initiative was judged to be successful, not just because it was effective in improving boys' performance in the KS2 reading SATs, but also because 'it was fun and enjoyable ... it became "cool" for boys to be seen reading and to give opinions on books', and because 'girls and boys valued each other's tastes in reading, fiction and non-fiction and different styles and genres'.

(www.standards.dfes.gov.uk/genderandachievement/goodpractice/primarycs/primarycs2)

Reading Journals

To overcome boys' reluctance to enter into discussion of personal responses to texts in the public setting of the classroom, interactive reading logs have proved very effective. Here boy readers can express their emotional reactions to books privately in a way that does not compromise their socially constructed masculine identity. When teachers are able to respond to pupils' comments in these journals, a two-way conversation about reading can develop. As Alison Street and Myra Barrs put it:

> Reading journals can be an important way of establishing the kind of discussion of books which boys find difficult to contribute to orally. They provide a space to explore experiences of books and stories. They can become real relationships on paper, where teacher and pupil establish a genuine dialogue about reading. (Barrs and Pidgeon, 1998: 9)

Reading diaries and letters addressed to the teacher about books read can work in the same way.

The advent of weblogs, or 'blogs', has added another dimension to this approach. It is well known that computer- and internet-related settings provide boys with an environment where they often feel more comfortable at expressing themselves, whether because of the anonymity this can provide or because new technology is seen as a male territory. Writing blogs about their reading has the same interactive potential for boys and their teachers as the traditional reading journal but also offers the opportunity for sharing responses with a wider audience of peers. Bloggers can assume a different identity online, if they wish, so that they can share their thoughts with others without being recognised personally. Online discussion groups can also enable boys to join in sharing of responses to books.

Literature Circles

As has been said, it takes two to read a book. In other words, until you have shared your responses with another reader you have not fully experienced the text. Journals and weblogs are valuable in enabling boys to join a virtual discussion of books and reading, and this is an important step. However, they do so by removing the physical presence of the reading community, with all the developmental benefits that a real social setting, rather than cyberspace, can bring. A way of successfully getting boys back into such a setting used by some schools is the literature circle. This has been defined as follows:

> In literature circles, children read and discuss a novel in small groups. Typically, literature circles are mixed ability and transient, formed to read and discuss a particular novel. The children choose the books they read and are wholly responsible for driving the group discussions. The teacher plays a crucial role in setting up and supporting each literature circle group but the emphasis is on the children taking responsibility. The literature circle discussion has a structured format but members of the group determine its content and direction. Each week, children read to their agreed target page at home and use previously taught strategies to remind themselves of the questions and observations they want to bring to their group discussion. After each meeting, pupils may be asked to write a response to the discussion and the group sets itself a new target page for the next week. When the book is finished, the group chooses a final presentation/review task from a list of possible activities suggested by the teacher. (Allan et al., 2005: 5)

This form of group reading has been well known for some time, but seems to have been more popular in the United States and, within the UK, in Scottish schools. Literature circles are certainly not intended only for boys nor only to benefit boy readers. They provide a way of developing the reading engagement and enjoyment of *all* children. However, the structure of the literature circle, as described above, does seem to have particular advantages for boys. In the report from which the above description comes, *Literature Circles, Gender and Reading for Enjoyment*, compiled for the Scottish Executive, the researchers asked four primary teachers to set up literature circles in their classrooms. The results demonstrated that all children in the groups gained a sense of autonomy and greater enthusiasm for reading, and this motivated them to want to set up other book discussion groups and to begin discussing their reading at home (Allan et al., 2005: 3). There were particular benefits for boys:

> Boys reported that they were more frequently reading for pleasure at home, recommending books to friends and getting totally absorbed in a book. These gains meant that the boys effectively 'caught up' with the girls in these aspects … The receptive vocabulary of the boys also improved. (p. 4)

Literature circles vary of course in how they are set up and run. Kathy Maclean, for example, gives an account of how literature circles were used with Year 4 pupils in a London primary school in the 1990s in a way that sounds closer to the guided reading promoted by the Primary National Strategy today, as discussed in Chapter 6. In these groups of inexperienced readers, the teacher had a more prominent role in choosing the texts, recapping the previous reading done and leading the discussion through questioning. The children also combined the use of reading journals with the literature circle, recording their thoughts and impressions about each text during the sessions. Again, the finding was that the support of the literature circle and the social interaction with other known readers benefited all the children but particularly helped to develop boys into more confident and reflective readers (Barrs and Pidgeon, 1998: 19–22).

More recently, Ruth Roberts (2006) has written about her use of literature circles with Year 6 pupils in a small rural primary school. Here the pupils spend 15–20 minutes each day working in self-selected groups of five to seven based on book choice. The emphasis is on self-direction but within a framework where pupils have group-defined roles such as 'the questioner', 'the summariser', 'the character tracker' and 'the next paragraph author' (p. 18). The teacher spends time with one group each week, but otherwise discussion is unsupervised. Roberts comments: 'Reading, talking, thinking, developing critical attitudes and learning collaboratively – the Literature Circle certainly covers several key areas in one neat package' (p. 18). Other ways of organising literature circles are discussed online (www.literaturecircles.com).

Reading Role Models

In response to the lack of role models of male readers mentioned above, some schools have devised imaginative ways of involving male family members and men in the local community in reading-related activities. For example, they have set up opportunities during the school day for involving fathers in 'Dads and Lads' book clubs, as mentioned in Chapter 2, or held special 'Grandads in School' days when grandfathers are encouraged to come in and promote reading with their grandsons. One primary school organised a reading week when fathers were invited to read a story of their choice to KS1 and a different one to KS2 children and to talk about their enjoyment of reading and the part that school had played in that (Bleach, 1998: 29–30).

Another popular strategy is to invite into school men who may be 'local heroes' on the sports field and use them as reading role models for boys, as in the school below.

Case Study School

This school was involved in the National Literacy Trust's *Kick into Reading* initiative with their local football club, the appropriately named Reading F.C. The local Schools Library Service did an assembly talk on the project and how children could be involved in a summer scheme of

(Continued)

(Continued)

which it was part. The school then took its Year 6 pupils along to storytelling sessions at the Central Library with the young Reading footballers. The subject leader reflected afterwards: 'It was very good, particularly for the boys, to see these young footballers promoting reading. Whether they, the boys, actually read more as a result would be quite difficult to gauge, but they're certainly more enthusiastic in talking about books'.

Reading F.C. has lived up to its name by, uniquely, training all its footballing apprentices in storytelling, so that they are able to present and create stories and poems to 8–12-year-olds in local schools, along with a professional storyteller. Parents have also been involved in two family workshop sessions to provide encouragement for family reading and storytelling. As Jim Sells, the Literacy Development Officer for the *Reading the Game* project, comments: 'The scheme provides positive male role models for reading at an age when traditionally children, and especially boys, are likely to begin reading less. The fact that the storytellers may be the same age as [the boys'] older brothers reinforces how reading can be cool'. (www.literacytrust.org.uk/Press/RTGReading)

The National Literacy Trust (NLT) also runs the wider *Reading the Game* initiative, working with well-known stars from professional football as well as cricket, tennis and wrestling 'to promote literacy and raise reading motivation for all ages'. As part of this, a *Reading the Game* DVD featuring sportsmen talking about reading has been made available to all English state schools and a Premier League Reading Stars scheme has involved setting up Saturday book clubs for readers, both boys and girls, 'who love football but might not love reading' (www.literacytrust.org.uk/Football). *Playing With Words* is a separate reading challenge run by the NLT designed to motivate older primary children, especially boys, 'to read for fun in their spare time'. Each class affiliated to the scheme has to read 100 books as a team over the course of one term, from reading lists provided, to qualify for a reward from their local football club.

In Lancashire, a local authority 'Dads and Lads' project has also tried to link reading with sporting activities to encourage fathers to become more involved in their child's literacy development. The scheme, aimed at boys aged between 4 and 13, involved dads taking home an item of sporting equipment from their son's school to practise a skill with them and also share a book or a poem about the same sport. The scheme has been developed to include 'Dads and Lads Rugby', the cricket-related 'Howzat Dads and Lads' and a football-based activity (www.lancashire.gov.uk).

Action Point

Think ahead to any major national or international sports event which will be held in the near future, such as European Championships, World Cups and Olympic Games. Brainstorm ways in which you could promote reading for enjoyment by linking it to these sporting events, for example by reading fiction, poetry and non-fiction related to different sports and sports personalities, setting up a 'Reading Olympics' for books or for readers, complete with medals, or reviewing Internet sites about the sports event. The theme of the 2008 Summer Reading Challenge in UK libraries is 'Sport' in order to exploits links with sports activities.

Reading Champions is another NLT initiative which is specifically intended to use 'the power of reading role models to inspire other men and boys to take up the reading habit' (www.literacytrust.co.uk/campaign/Champions). This is a project aimed at males of all ages, but there is a specific School Reading Champions scheme whereby boys can engage in reading promotion activities at different levels, from writing book reviews to organising a school book event, and earn bronze, silver and gold awards. The Reading Champions are not only keen readers themselves, but men and boys within the school who actively get others involved in reading for pleasure. A *Reading Champions Toolkit,* specifically written for schools to help them set up their own schemes, is available from the NLT website (with a cover that resembles a Haynes car repair manual). To make sure the girls do not feel left out, there is also a separate *Reading Angels* scheme, though without the same external recognition in the form of certificates and badges: possibly some unintended messages about gender here!

As well as boys who already have an interest in reading, some schools have targeted a different group to become reading ambassadors. These are boys who, for various reasons, have status in the eyes of other pupils as leaders or trendsetters. The idea is that reading can become a 'cool' activity by being associated with this influential grouping. One school issued a group of boys of this kind with pink T-shirts to announce their love of reading and to indicate their role in inspiring their classmates to enjoy reading, in this case reading newspapers. Within a month, the (dark!) pink T-shirts had become the most sought-after fashion accessory in the school; the pink-shirted boys regularly read out newspaper articles in assemblies, and other boys aspired to join this elite reading cohort. Whether being 'proud to wear pink' and 'man enough to admit you like reading' is challenging or reinforcing gender stereotypes is problematic, but the initiative certainly had a positive impact on boys' behaviour and confidence, according to the teacher concerned (Bishop, 2006: 5).

More recently the NLT has supported the launch of Star Reads in conjunction with the online bookstore Passionet. This organisation has a commitment to developing reading in schools and communities, as expressed on its website: 'We recognise that society has become more culturally diverse and remain committed to offering books with subjects and topics of interest to young people, which will fuel their enthusiasm for reading. At Passionet we realise how important it is to get urban youth excited, inspired and motivated to read' (www.starreads.org). For Black History Month in October 2006, the website launched a series of posters of 'five of today's most influential UK urban role models', including rappers, singers, actors and DJs, recommending their favourite books. The campaign has a particular focus on black, urban youth, and is obviously not aimed at just boys, but four of the five Star Readers are men, and the website has a clear appeal for boys.

Most recently the NLT has published a magazine *Getting the Blokes on Board* (2007), which includes case studies of how early years settings, primary and secondary schools have engaged fathers and male carers in reading with their children both in and out of the classroom. These include 'Bring a Dad to School' weeks, 'Fun for Fathers' evenings of book-based activities, themed reading days involving the local library, and short training sessions for men on story reading and storytelling. The magazine, downloadable from the NLT website, also includes evidence from research about the bene-fits of involving dads and practical tips for how schools can begin to develop involvement. There are also features on involving fathers in their children's reading through other settings such as prisons, libraries and football clubs (www.literacytrust.org.uk).

Jackie Marsh has described other successful strategies which have been used to involve fathers in children's reading development in the primary school:

- encouraging fathers and children to visit football grounds together and note down environmental print found there, taking photographs and later making books about their visit;
- creating a home–school comic lending library to encourage fathers to share comics with their children;
- asking dads to make books about their interests and hobbies for their children;
- making a wall display of 'Dads' Favourite Books', using book covers and thought-bubbles to give fathers' responses to the texts;
- setting up a 'Curiosity Kits' lending scheme, on the model of 'Story Sacks', using non-fiction books and related artefacts, to develop book-sharing between fathers and children;
- using experienced male parents as 'parent buddies' to mentor new parents in supporting their children's reading.
  (in Lewis and Ellis, 2006: 68–69)

Sometimes the male reading models for boys can be provided by older pupils from the same primary school or from local secondary schools. Reading bud-dies, as mentioned above, have been shown to be effective in promoting and developing reading for all children and have benefits for the older children as well as for the junior partners in terms of building confidence, self-esteem and motivation. Boys in particular seem to benefit from having other boys as reading buddies, as in the school below. Training is important, though, as Colin Noble has shown, so that the older pupils are aware of how and how not to approach their mentoring role (Bleach 1998: 26–27).

Case Study School

This primary school has been involved through the local Schools Library Service in shadowing the Kate Greenaway Medal for a number of years. This year they developed further an existing sports-based link with a nearby boys' secondary school so that a number of Year 8 boys (12–13 years) came in and did work on the shortlisted books with Year 5 and Year 2 pupils. There was also a visit to the library at the boys' school for some activities on the books. The school's English subject leader commented: 'This has been very successful, a good activity for getting the primary school boys as well as the secondary ones involved in reading, and the school will definitely continue with it in future years'.

As well as this kind of pupil mentoring, book-related websites run by their peers are useful in motivating boys to read and review books for enjoyment. For example, www.cool-reads.co.uk is a popular site where 'books for 10–15-year-old readers are reviewed by 10–15-year-old reviewers', in various categories of genre and theme. Founded by two boys, Chris and Tim, when they were in this age-range, and containing many reviews by them, the website has a particular appeal for boys and provides a good model for them to follow for Internet reviewing. Another website with book recommendations and dedicated to encouraging boys to read is the children's author Jon Szceiska's site (www.guysread.com). This American site is more anarchic, child-friendly and seemingly 'non-educational' in approach, very like Jon Szceiska's own books. By contrast another American site aimed at getting boys reading, www.geocities.com/talestoldtall, run by storyteller and children's author Michael Sullivan, has a much clearer educational emphasis, with articles and books for teachers.

Through all these ways of involving male readers as role models runs an *implicit* challenge to the 'laddish' attitudes and 'anti-swot' culture which prevent many boys from engaging with reading, along with other aspects of learning. In addition to the initiatives and activities mentioned above, there may be times when it is necessary also to *explicitly* confront this form of street-culture where it is prevalent in the local community, through personalised or group discussion and activities with boys which can involve fathers and older brothers.

Interactive Whiteboards

Many teachers I spoke to in my research mentioned interactive whiteboards (IWBs), linked to laptop computers and data projectors, as a medium for sharing texts with the whole class which was motivating for all readers, but which helped to stimulate boys' interest in reading in particular.

Many of the electronic texts being used with these boards were certainly boy-friendly ones, such as adventure, space and spy stories. For example the popular Longman Digitexts series, used by many of the teachers in my research, featured titles with boy-appeal such as *Feargal Fly: Private Eye,* a detective story by Louise Glasspoole; *The Lost Boy* by Louise Cooper, a mystery story; a futuristic adventure, *Last Mission* by Adam Gullain; and a space story *Danger! Monster! Aliens!* by Andrea Shavick. But the key to the success of these digital texts seemed to be their *interactivity*, that reading the texts involved pupils doing things rather than passively listening to the teacher read them, and this appealed to boys in particular. The interactivity also involved discussion between pupils, and between pupils and teachers, related to the digital texts. The texts themselves were non-linear fiction and non-fiction, which encouraged group involvement with the text through decision-making and problem-solving of a kind similar to the Choose-Your-Own Adventure books of the pre-digital era. Without this element of inter-action, the activity easily became a passive one itself, akin to watching a very large television screen.

One teacher I interviewed described the IWB as 'one of the most exciting things that's happened for a long time in teaching reading', and 'one of those learning experiences where it's going to take years to become completely familiar with everything that's available to you'. Sharing interactive stories through the IWB, when children physically came up to the screen and manipulated text, images, animations, music and sounds, was a very exciting way of drawing children in, particularly those not used to having text in front of them, she believed. This teacher felt strongly that the IWB kept children, especially boys, much more on task than an equivalent print-based Big Book would do.

Overall, the consensus of the teachers I interviewed was that the potential of IWBs and electronic texts to be an effective way of engaging boys in shared reading was probably best realised when the activity demonstrated some of the following features:

- It was a collaborative activity involving the whole class and/or small groups, which promoted dialogue between pupils.
- It encouraged pupil autonomy in decision-making.
- It was presented in achievable chunks.
- It was clearly structured.
- It contained elements of challenge.
- It encouraged creative thinking.
- It provided opportunities for the use of different learning styles.
- It got off to a brisk start and developed momentum.

Case Study School

Finally, one Year 6 teacher reported a positive effect of gender difference on reading in her school, which she was actively encouraging. A growing number of boys were taking Jacqueline Wilson books out of the school library, she noticed, in order to make themselves more appealing to the girls in their year group. Perhaps this is the ultimate way to get boys engaged with books: as a way of increasing their attractiveness to the opposite sex!

Action Point

Take one of the ideas or activities suggested in this chapter for developing boys' reading for pleasure in the primary school. Plan how you could incorporate it into your teaching and how you could evaluate its effectiveness afterwards. How would you avoid any detrimental effect on girls' motivation and attitude?

Chapter **6**

Conclusions

Summary

Chapter 6 draws on findings from the author's research project to discuss possible starting points for schools seeking to develop reading for pleasure in their whole school communities. It then summarises the factors which this research concludes are significant for schools to develop reading for enjoyment further. Finally, two important factors from the ones listed are focused on: teachers' knowledge of children's books and teachers' approaches to national literacy frameworks and related assessment tests.

Where to Start

At the end of my interviews with each of the English subject leaders I spoke to during my research, I asked the same question: *What would be the first things you would recommend a school to do in order to develop a successful reading for pleasure culture?* The replies from these teachers, all of whom had established very positive attitudes to reading amongst the children in their schools, revealed a lot of agreement about what elements needed to be developed and where they wanted to end up. However, there were different starting points.

Starting with the whole school

Some of the subject leaders felt the best place to begin was by looking across the whole school to try to ascertain why it *did not* have a reading for pleasure culture in the first place and to assess where the school was in terms of reading engagement. One of the first initiatives would then be staff training, both within school and in centres of excellence elsewhere, to introduce teachers and teaching assistants to techniques and strategies for improving children's attitudes to reading. There would then be a thorough reassessment of the role of the school library and the classroom libraries to make them more visible in promoting reading for enjoyment. Thirdly there would be whole-school events to raise the profile of reading, such as teacher- or pupil-led assemblies about reading, book weeks, book days, readathons and visits by authors or by 'local heroes' from the wider school community.

Starting with parents

For other subject leaders, it was parents and carers who were the key. As one teacher put it, 'without parents there, you are missing a whole link. I feel very strongly that the parents would be where I'd begin'. This would mean holding parents' meetings and workshops, as the first step, preferably combined with author visits or book events, such as quizzes, to hook in as many family members as possible. Parents would need to be recruited to help support reading for enjoyment both at home and within school, with their own children and with others. Clear and realistic proposals would be needed to get parents on board at the outset and to involve them as much as possible in planning reading promotion initiatives, with a particular emphasis on attracting fathers and male carers through appropriate opportunities and activities.

Starting with your own class

For quite a number of the subject leaders, though, the best place to start was in their own classroom with the teaching groups they taught there. This would mean fact-finding with their own class first and diagnosing where they were in terms of reading engagement, introducing tried and tested books as read alouds for the whole class, and then gradually introducing more time for independent wider reading. 'Always start at a small level,' as one teacher said, 'make sure that your class is enjoying reading, make sure that you personally have a good supply of good-quality books, and talk about books in your everyday conversations.' The message about promoting the pleasures of reading would then be spread to other teachers through an approach that stressed 'making your life easier' as a reading teacher by using good-quality books not textbooks. This softly-softly campaign would be more of 'a snowball', as one teacher put it, gradually gathering momentum, rather than a sudden icy blast. From other teachers and their classes, this campaign would then gently spread to involve parents and carers.

For almost all of the subject leaders, whatever their starting point, modelling good reading behaviour and practice in some way to other teachers, to children and to parents was crucial. This meant showing enthusiasm for reading and for teaching reading, which spread a vital spark to others. Often teachers used metaphors of fire or battle in their comments about their own teaching approach, 'igniting a flame', as one teacher put it, through the use of drama, storytelling and oral activities as a prelude to reading texts in her case. Another teacher talked about 'attacking literacy lessons with enjoyment, the reading, the drama, the speaking and listening; really getting them to enjoy their texts because once they do that, they want to read, and I think if you can get the children, that gets their parents as well'.

> ### Pause for Thought
>
> Of the three starting points above for developing a reading culture in a school to which you are newly appointed, which one would you favour and why? Would you prefer to combine the three in some way? Or would you take a different starting point altogether?

What Factors are Important?

Once a beginning has been made, from whichever starting point is decided on, what factors are then important in the development of reading for pleasure in the primary school? From the interviews, questionnaires and observations I carried out for my research, as discussed in the preceding chapters, a number of factors have emerged as significant in the reading classroom itself:

- Teachers having good knowledge and understanding of the full range of children's literature.
- Teachers being able to use national literacy frameworks flexibly and creatively.
- Teachers having good knowledge and understanding of their pupils' reading choices, tastes and preferences.
- Teachers providing a positive role model as enthusiastic readers.
- Teachers using open-ended, authentic activities rather than closed-off, artificial ones, such as the completion of textbook exercises or worksheets.
- Teachers using active approaches to exploring and responding to texts, involving the use of drama and other creative arts.
- Teachers using a range of reading material, both print and electronic, and valuing pupils' own reading choices.
- Teachers making use of interactive whiteboards to encourage pupils, particularly boys, to engage with texts.
- Teachers making use of Internet formats such as weblogs to involve pupils, particularly boys, in responding to texts.
- Pupils being able to exercise autonomy and choice in some reading activities.
- Pupils being able to collaborate in groups and interact with others during some reading activities.
- A classroom environment that contains appropriate and interesting texts, which are accessible and attractively displayed.

In addition to these features of successful reading for pleasure classrooms, my research findings have also suggested the importance of the following factors in promoting reading for enjoyment more widely within the primary school as a whole:

- Having a regular timetabled slot where teachers read aloud to pupils.
- Having a regular timetabled slot where pupils read independently.
- Involving parents and other adults in the local community fully in supporting reading within the school and at home for all age-groups.
- Using library resources in the school and local community fully and developing links between the two.
- Involving pupils fully in the provision of books in the school through ordering and stock-taking.
- Having an incentive scheme to reward achievements in reading which reflects the value of the activity.
- Taking part in national initiatives and networks to promote reading for pleasure, such as those run by the National Literacy Trust.
- Running extra-curricular reading/book clubs for pupils at lunchtime or after school.
- Developing a culture of 'book talk' within the school, so that conversations about reading become the norm.
- Seeing reading for pleasure as part of a wider 'learning for pleasure' curriculum and developing learners and readers 'for life'.

Most of these factors have been discussed and illustrated at length in the chapters above, which have highlighted good practice in successful schools. However, more needs to be said in conclusion about the two factors at the head of the first list on p. 118, which are particularly important, and which were mentioned by all those primary subject leaders I spoke to in the interviews I carried out for my research project. I quote from their responses below.

Teachers having good knowledge and understanding of the full range of children's literature

Nearly 40 years ago the author and pioneer of the study and teaching of children's literature, Aidan Chambers, put forward the view that:

> The effectiveness of any teacher in the encouragement of the reading habit varies in proportion to the teacher's depth of knowledge of children's books and literature generally ... The teacher who reads avidly [herself or] himself, the teacher who knows and reads children's books, invariably fosters a similar interest in a high percentage of [her or] his pupils. (Chambers, 1969: 117)

However, Chambers also felt at the time that:

> ... the teaching profession is a profession of reluctant readers ... They are rarely seen to read a novel, purr over it with pleasure, dwell on it with interest, talk about it with enthusiasm or anger; worse, they are never seen even carrying one. They are seen with chalky textbooks. They are heard hacking a set-book to pieces. (Chambers, 1969: 117)

For this reason, Chambers argued strongly for teachers' (and librarians') pre-service training to include courses in children's literature. He later estimated that the optimum number of books primary school teachers needed to know at the start of their careers in order to function satisfactorily in the classroom 'hovers around the five hundred mark' (Chambers, 1993: 16).

Recent research has suggested that many teachers' knowledge of children's literature is still limited, particularly compared with this expectation. A recent survey of 1200 primary teachers for a United Kingdom Literacy Association project on 'Teachers as Readers' found, for example, that while the majority of primary teachers could name six children's authors when asked, most could not name more than three poets for children and over 20% could not name a single one. There were gaps in primary teachers' knowledge of picture books, too: the majority could not name more than three picture book authors and almost 25% were not able to name one (Ward, 2007: 14). The researchers found these numbers 'worrying, particularly with regard to teachers' capacity to make recommendations to independent readers'. However, 70% of the teachers did report reading for pleasure themselves in the month before the survey, although the researchers felt that there was a discrepancy here: 'while the teachers' personal adult reading covered a wide range of authors, topics and types of books, the texts used in the classroom were drawn from a much narrower range,' often light, fun texts only. Teachers could be more adventurous with their classroom choices, it was felt (Cremin et al., 2007: 25).

In addition, a recent government-funded initiative to involve librarians in teaching children's literature on Initial Teacher Training courses suggested that there was concern that graduates have insufficient knowledge of children's books when they enter the profession:

> The Arts Council, in their 2003 consultation paper on children's literature, *From Looking Glass to Spyglass*, identified that there is no statutory requirement for trainee teachers to study children's literature. For many, this has been a cause for concern, especially when viewed against the growing evidence base demonstrating that many teachers are not confident in promoting children's books, that they are failing to use the expertise of children's and school libraries and that they lack awareness of children's literature. (Museums, Libraries and Archives Council, 2005)

The overwhelming majority of the subject leaders I surveyed who were successfully promoting the enjoyment of reading in their schools had good or very good knowledge and understanding of children's books, and felt that it was important to develop this awareness in other teaching staff. They all read for pleasure themselves, both children's and adult books (except for one respondent who was also the acting headteacher and sadly had time to read only official documents now), and most remembered enjoying reading as a child. Some had specialised in children's literature during their initial training and had continued to keep up with children's books since then. Some were currently studying for further qualifications, such as Masters degrees, in this area. For others, their interest in and awareness of children's books had been developed on the job, through in-service training, through personal interest arising out of their teaching, or through informal mentoring by a more knowledgeable colleague. All were now in a position where, as subject leaders, they could advise and support other teachers in their choice of texts and seek to enthuse them as readers of children's literature. All saw this as a necessary and important part of their role in nurturing the reading habit within their schools.

One subject leader was insistent that all the teachers in her school now read books themselves from start to finish before they read them to the children, something which had not always happened before she took up the role: 'we have looked at this as a whole school and decided that it is important because our enthusiasm comes through to the children, and if you enjoy a book the children are a lot more willing to be involved in it.' As another subject leader pointed out: 'I don't know how you would pick a good exciting text to use in a lesson if you didn't really have a good bank of knowledge about texts'. Teachers needed to be confident in their ability to help children in making appropriate reading choices through their knowledge of what was available, either from their own personal and professional reading or from knowing where to look for advice and recommendations (see Resources in Chapter 7). Without this confidence, as most of my interviewees pointed out, it would be difficult for teachers to promote reading to pupils as an entertaining and rewarding activity.

Teachers being able to use national literacy frameworks flexibly and creatively

'You can put barriers in the way if you want to, but if you really want something, you can make sure it fits, that's just how I feel,' was one subject leader's comment on her approach to the original National Literacy Strategy framework, which echoed that of the majority of others I interviewed. The literacy objectives from the framework *could* be used to promote reading for pleasure, but you needed to know the children and the texts very well, and use the objectives creatively to fit what you as a teacher actually wanted to do. Most of these subject leaders had not used the structure of the Literacy Hour strictly even from the beginning (only 8% of the 40 surveyed) and had used it increasingly flexibly over time.

For some teachers, the NLS and its Literacy Hour were actually useful dis-ciplines which it was necessary to go through so that they could discover its limitations. As one subject leader put it:

> I do believe quite strongly that using the strategy is something that all staff need to have gone through before they can then take the ownership and say, 'Actually, hang on a minute, for this group of pupils this doesn't work, I need to be doing this, this and this'. So we spent a couple of years really ensuring that everyone had that as part of their being. Over the past two or three years staff have now started to realise that although yes, it is important that we have to meet the needs of the literacy documents that are out there, it is also really doubly impor-tant that we meet the needs of the pupils that are in our care. You need to go through it [the NLS] to be able to say this is the reason why I'm *not* doing it.

However, there was also recognition that the NLS and Literacy Hour struc-tures could be restricting and intimidating for teachers who were not English specialists or who were younger teachers who had never know anything other than the NLS framework. For these teachers, is was harder to bend the frame-work objectives to their own aims and to think outside the Literacy Hour box. The NLS could become a comfort zone, a teaching frame that told you what to do or even what to say and what questions to ask, on which teachers could become too reliant.

There was one element of the original NLS and Literacy Hour which the teachers I interviewed had come to view as a valuable part of their practice in engaging children in reading and this was guided reading. Initially widely ignored as part of group work within the recommended Literacy Hour struc-ture, guided reading had eventually found a home in many of my sample schools outside the Hour and become an important element in the reading curriculum, where it sat between whole-class shared reading and individual independent reading. Guided reading, as practised in most of the successful schools I visited, involved children working in ability groups and reading texts that were at instructional level for them, under the guidance of the teacher or teaching assistant. As one of my interviewees pointed out, guided reading was 'not all about the children reading', and in fact often involved more discussion than anything else, with reading being done independently at other times. At its worst, some felt, guided reading could become an overly formal, almost scripted encounter between teachers, children and texts, particularly where the adults were not confident in their knowledge of children's books. At their best, though, teachers reported that guided reading sessions became focused and intensive explorations of both fiction and non-fiction books which gave children opportunities to develop real collective engagement with texts and teachers the chance to communicate their enthusiasm for books and reading.

The English subject leaders I spoke to broadly welcomed the renewed *Framework* (DfES, 2006a) for Literacy, with its fewer objectives, less prescrip-tive approach, integration of oral activities into literacy teaching, and longer units of teaching time. However, they recognised that this greater freedom brought its own challenges, especially for those teachers who had never taught prior to the original NLS.

For other teachers, though, reading for pleasure could only ever really take place outside of the Literacy Hour or other structured lessons, in read aloud or silent reading time:

> I think reading for pleasure is more about enjoying a story, listening to a story, engaging with a story, imagining yourself in a story. You don't do that that much with texts that you share because you're going at quite a pace as well. Reading for pleasure is quite personal in a way. You can do it with a friend or you can do it with a whole class, but it's about just enjoying a book for the book, not for whether it's got how many full stops or are there words beginning with 'Sh' or whatever.

Whereas the subject leaders I interviewed felt they were able to adapt the literacy curriculum to their own purposes in the promotion of reading in particular, the Standard Assessment Tests (SATs), administered nationally at ages 7 and 11, were seen by the majority as constricting and sometimes actually distorting their teaching. A minority of teachers, though, refused to adapt their approach in favour of coaching for the tests, arguing that their normal reading teaching was actually better preparation. As one teacher put it, 'how better to get children to achieve a really good reading comprehension mark than getting them to empathise with characters in stories they've read?', or in the words of another, 'the children think they're just chatting about a book but they're actually preparing for answering SATs comprehension questions'.

However, one Year 2 teacher vividly illustrated the pressures most felt in preparing children for the SATs reading tasks at age 7 when she described her typical thought processes: 'what level are you on now and what do I need to do to get you up to the next one, despite the fact of whether you are enjoying it or not? And we can't talk about this now, dear, because we need to work out how we're going to tackle this …' The pressures of this results-driven, 'high-stakes' testing of reading were felt by parents as well as schools, as another teacher described:

> The SATs at KS1 create a problem amongst parents. They are very worried about it and their children are only 6 years old. There is a lot more pressure now on young children in terms of what level a child is at, pressure that could detract from their enjoyment of reading. Just reading to your child is enough, but many parents feel the need to buy commercial revision guides to help with reading.

At Year 6 (age 10–11) the feeling of most of my interviewees was also that SATs got in the way of reading for enjoyment. Many of the teachers I spoke to felt they had to prepare KS2 children for things not taught yet, because they were not in the curriculum until after SATs. Having to juggle the reading curriculum so it fitted in with SATs meant it became contrived. The content of the reading tests was also criticised as 'boring', sometimes ambiguous in terms of demands made on inference and deduction in reading comprehension, with questions that would be 'taxing for some adults'.

Teachers described trying to minimise pressure on children and the amount of time spent on test preparation, but felt it definitely distorted things. This echoes a survey conducted by the QCA which, according to a report in the *Times Educational Supplement* (*TES*), found that teachers spent nearly half the week on SATs preparation from January to May of Year 6 and some reported starting test preparation in Year 5. The Head of the QCA is quoted as commenting on these statistics:

> Too much attention is being given to preparing for tests and practising doing them ... there is a difference between good teaching and cramming. If schools are replacing classroom lessons with preparation for a test that might be months or weeks away, I think the priorities are wrong.

However, as the *TES* report concludes, many schools and teachers say they have little option but to drill pupils for months, given the demands of government league tables and targets on which their performance is ultimately judged (Mansell and Ward, 2007). Pupils seem to agree that SATs preparation has a negative impact on their learning in literacy, as Ofsted (2005) reported: 'most pupils continue to have positive views about their English lessons, although they tell inspectors that over-preparation for the national tests reduces their enjoyment.' This seems to be a factor that will continue to inhibit the efforts of many primary schools to promote reading for enjoyment without a change in the direction of UK government policy on national assessment.

Pause for Thought

Is it possible to follow official curriculum and assessment requirements and still help children discover the pleasures of reading? Or is it necessary to go outside these restrictions or to subvert them in some way?

Final Thoughts

The teaching of reading in primary schools has always been a controversial subject and will remain so. It is not for nothing that the term 'reading wars' is often used to characterise this debate. Whether it is prompted by concern about standards of reading attainment or about levels of reading motivation, this conflict will continue as long as schools teach reading. Different interest groups, whether in the fields of politics, education, publishing or the print and broadcasting media, will pursue their own entrenched positions, often regardless of the evidence of research.

This was brought home to me vividly by the press coverage of an earlier, interim account of my research in a teachers' journal (Lockwood, 2007). Although the article presented a positive view overall of children's attitudes to reading in the schools I surveyed, a review in one particular newspaper homed in solely on the negative comments of some of the children. The headline read, 'READING IS FOR THE "NERDS" SAY CHILDREN' and the review began, 'Settling down to a good book is for "nerds" and libraries are boring, say pupils in a major survey of children's reading habits' (Henry, 2007). I hope that the account given here paints a fuller and more encouraging picture than that of how schools are able to promote reading for pleasure and how children respond.

Chapter 7

Resources for Promoting Reading for Pleasure

Creating a Reading for Pleasure Library

Any library should reflect the reader or readers' own tastes. The lists of children's picture books, novels and poetry below are a personal selection of books I've enjoyed and are not a definitive guide. I hope they will be useful to the non-specialist and to teachers who want to develop their awareness of children's literature. Specialists will already have their own, no doubt quite different, lists. I've limited myself to 100 titles in each category, including only the first book of any series. The suggested age-ranges are, as ever, a very rough guide only, and are not meant to imply that younger or older readers cannot also enjoy the books. Non-fiction books are not included here as the range of possible topics would be too great.

Picture books

5–7

Alan Durant and Vanessa Cabban, *Dear Tooth Fairy* (Walker)
Anthony Browne, *Bear Hunt* (Hamish Hamilton)
Anthony Browne, *Through the Magic Mirror* (Hamish Hamilton)
Anthony Browne, *Willy and Hugh* (Red Fox)
Anthony Browne, *Willy the Champ* (Walker)
Anthony Browne, *Willy the Wimp* (Walker)
Babette Cole, *Princess Smartypants* (Puffin)
Colin McNaughton and Satoshi Kitamura, *Once Upon an Ordinary School Day* (Andersen Press)
Colin McNaughton, *Suddenly!* (Andersen Press)
Cressida Cowell and Neal Layton, *That Rabbit Belongs to Emily Brown* (Orchard)
Cressida Cowell, *Little Bo Peep's Library Book* (Hodder)
David McKee, *Not Now, Bernard* (Andersen Press)

David McKee, *The Conquerors* (Andersen Press)
David McKee, *Tusk Tusk* (Andersen Press)
David McKee, *Two Monsters* (Andersen Press)
Eileen Browne, *Handa's Surprise* (Walker)
Emily Gravett, *Wolves* (Macmillan)
Eugene Trivizas and Helen Oxenbury, *The Three Little Wolves and the Big Bad Pig* (Egmont)
Giles Andreae and Guy Parker-Rees, *Giraffes Can't Dance* (Orchard)
Helen Cooper, *Pumpkin Soup* (Doubleday)
Helen Cooper, *The Bear under the Stairs* (Doubleday)
Hiawyn Oram and Satoshi Kitamura, *Angry Arthur* (Red Fox)
Inga Moore, *Six-Dinner Sid* (Hodder)
Jan Ormerod, *Moonlight* (Kestrel)
Jan Ormerod, *Sunshine* (Kestrel)
Jill Murphy, *On the Way Home* (Macmillan)
Jill Murphy, *Peace at Last* (Macmillan)
John Burningham, *Come Away from the Water, Shirley* (Cape)
John Burningham, *Granpa* (Cape)
John Burningham, *Where's Julius?* (Cape)
John Burningham, *Would You Rather ...* (Cape)
Judith Kerr, *The Tiger Who Came to Tea* (Collins)
Judy Sierra and Marc Brown, *Wild About Books* (Frances Lincoln)
Julia Donaldson and Axel Scheffler, *The Gruffalo* (Macmillan)
Lauren Child, *Beware of the Storybook Wolves* (Hodder)
Lauren Child, *Who's Afraid of the Big Bad Book?* (Hodder)
Lauren Child, *Clarice Bean, That's Me!* (Orchard)
Lynley Dodd, *Hairy Maclary from Donaldson's Dairy* (Viking)
Mairi Hedderwick, *Katie Morag Delivers the Mail* (Bodley Head)
Martin Waddell and Barbara Firth, *Can't You Sleep, Little Bear?* (Walker)
Martin Waddell and Patrick Benson, *Owl Babies* (Walker)
Mary Hoffman and Caroline Binch, *Amazing Grace* (Frances Lincoln)
Mary Hoffman and Karin Littlewood, *The Colour of Home* (Frances Lincoln)
Maurice Sendak, *Where the Wild Things Are* (Bodley Head)
Max Velthuijs, *Frog in Love* (Andersen Press)
Michael Rosen and Helen Oxenbury, *We're Going on a Bear Hunt* (Walker)
Nick Butterworth, *The Whisperer* (HarperCollins)
Nikolai Popov, *Why?* (North-South Books)
Nicholas Allen, *Jesus' Christmas Party* (Hutchinson)
Oliver Jeffers, *The Incredible Book Eating Boy* (HarperCollins)
Pat Hutchins, *Rosie's Walk* (Bodley Head)
Peter Collington, *On Christmas Eve* (Heinemann)
Quentin Blake, *Clown* (Cape)
Raymond Briggs, *The Snowman* (Hamish Hamilton)
Shirley Hughes, *Alfie Gets in First* (Red Fox)
Shirley Hughes, *Dogger* (Bodley Head)

Shirley Hughes, *Up and Up* (Bodley Head)
Ted Dewan, *The Pig Who Had It All* (Corgi)

7–9

Allan and Janet Ahlberg, *The Jolly Postman: or Other People's Letters* (Viking)
Anthony Browne, *Gorilla* (Julia MacRae)
Anthony Browne, *Hansel and Gretel* (Julia MacRae)
Anthony Browne, *My Dad* (Doubleday)
Anthony Browne, *Piggybook* (Julia MacRae)
Anthony Browne, *Voices in the Park* (Doubleday)
Anthony Browne, *Zoo* (Julia MacRae)
Babette Cole, *Drop Dead* (Red Fox)
Babette Cole, *Hair in Funny Places* (Cape)
Babette Cole, *Mummy Laid an Egg* (Red Fox)
Fiona French, *Snow White in New York* (Oxford)
Jeanne Willis and Tony Ross, *Dr Xargle's Book of Earthlets* (Andersen Press)
Jenny Wagner and Ron Brooks, *John Brown, Rose and the Midnight Cat* (Kestrel)
Jon Scieszka and Lane Smith, *The True Story of the Three Little Pigs* (Puffin)
Jon Scieszka and Steve Johnson, *The Frog Prince Continued* (Puffin)
Raymond Briggs, *The Bear* (Julia MacRae)
Russell Hoban and Quentin Blake, *How Tom Beat Captain Najork and his Hired Sportsmen* (Cape)
Sarah Stewart and David Small *The Library* (Frances Lincoln)
Susan Varley, *Badger's Parting Gifts* (Andersen Press)

9–11

Anthony Browne, *King Kong* (Julia MacRae)
Chris Van Allsburg, *The Mysteries of Harris Burdick* (Andersen Press)
Chris Van Allsburg, *The Widow's Broom* (Andersen Press)
Gary Crew and Shaun Tan, *Memorial* (Lothian Children's Books)
Jon Scieszka and Lane Smith, *The Stinky Cheese Man and Other Fairly Stupid Tales* (Puffin)
Junko Morimoto, *My Hiroshima* (Puffin)
Libby Hathorn and Gregory Rogers, *Way Home* (Andersen Press)
Michael Foreman, *After the War Was Over* (Pavilion Books)
Michael Foreman, *War and Peas* (Andersen Press)
Michael Foreman, *War Boy* (Pavilion)
Michael Foreman, *War Game* (Pavilion)
Michael Foreman, *Dinosaurs and All that Rubbish* (Puffin)
Michael Rosen and Quentin Blake, *Michael Rosen's Sad Book* (Walker)
Raymond Briggs, *Ethel and Ernest: A True Story* (Cape)
Raymond Briggs, *Fungus the Bogeyman* (Hamish Hamilton)
Raymond Briggs, *The Man* (Julia MacRae)

Raymond Briggs, *The Tin-Pot Foreign General and the Old Iron Woman* (Hamish Hamilton)
Raymond Briggs, *When the Wind Blows* (Hamish Hamilton)
Roberto Innocento and Ruth Vander Zee, *Erika's Story* (Cape)
Roberto Innocento, translated by Ian McEwan, *Rose Blanche* (Cape)
Shirley Hughes, *The Lion and the Unicorn* (Red Fox)
Susan Wojciechowski and P.J. Lynch, *The Christmas Miracle of Jonathan Toomey* (Walker)

Novels

5–7

Allan Ahlberg and Katherine McEwen, *The Cat Who Got Carried Away* (Walker)
Allan Ahlberg and Katherine McEwen, *The Children Who Smelled a Rat* (Walker)
Allan Ahlberg and Katherine McEwen, *The Man Who Wore All His Clothes* (Walker)
Allan Ahlberg and Katherine McEwen, *The Woman Who Won Things* (Walker)
Arnold Lobel, *Frog and Toad Are Friends* (HarperCollins)
Dick King-Smith, *The Hodgeheg* (Hamish Hamilton)
Florence Parry Heide and Edward Gorey, *The Shrinking of Treehorn* (Puffin)
Georgie Adams and Emily Bolam, *The Three Little Witches Storybook* (Orion)
Ian Whybrow and Tony Ross, *Little Wolf's Book of Badness* (Collins)
Jeff Brown and Scott Nash, *Flat Stanley* (Egmont)
Joyce Dunbar, *The Ups and Downs of Mouse and Mole* (Corgi)
Roald Dahl and Quentin Blake, *The Magic Finger* (Puffin)

7–9

Andrew Clements, *Frindle* (Simon and Schuster)
Andy Stanton, *You're a Bad Man, Mr Gum!* (Egmont)
Anne Fine, *Bill's New Frock* (Methuen)
Anne Fine, *Diary of a Killer Cat* (Puffin)
Clive King, *Stig of the Dump* (Puffin)
Cressida Cowell, *How to Train Your Dragon* (Hodder)
David Almond, *My Dad's a Birdman* (Walker)
Dick King-Smith, *George Speaks* (Puffin)
Dick King-Smith, *The Fox Busters* (Puffin)
Dick King-Smith, *The Sheep Pig* (Gollancz)
E.B. White, *Charlotte's Web* (Puffin)
Eoin Colfer, *The Legend of Spud Murphy* (Puffin)
Francesca Simon, *Horrid Henry* (Orion)
Geraldine McCaughrean, *Smile!* (Oxford)
Humphrey Carpenter, *Mr Majeika* (Puffin)
Jacqueline Wilson, *Lizzie Zipmouth* (Random House)
Jacqueline Wilson, *The Story of Tracy Beaker* (Doubleday)
Jenny Nimmo, *The Owl Tree* (Walker)

Jeremy Strong, *The Karate Princess* (Puffin)
Jill Murphy, *The Worst Witch* (Puffin)
Jill Tomlinson, *The Owl Who Was Afraid of the Dark* (Egmont)
Lauren Child, *Utterly Me, Clarice Bean* (Orchard)
Michael Morpurgo and Christian Birmingham, *The Butterfly Lion* (Collins)
Michael Morpurgo and Michael Foreman, *Billy the Kid* (Collins)
Michael Morpurgo and Michael Foreman, *Cool!* (Collins)
Paul Stewart and Chris Riddell, *Fergus Crane* (Doubleday)
Paul Stewart and Chris Riddell, *Muddle Earth* (Macmillan)
Pete Johnson, *Rescuing Dad* (Random House)
Philip Pullman, *I Was a Rat or The Scarlet Slippers* (Corgi)
Philip Pullman, *The Firework-Maker's Daughter* (Doubleday)
Philippa Pearce, *The Battle of Bubble and Squeak* (Puffin)
Roald Dahl, *Fantastic Mr Fox* (Puffin)
Roald Dahl, *George's Marvellous Medicine* (Puffin)
Robert Swindells, *The Ice Palace* (Hamish Hamilton)
Shirley Hughes, *Chips and Jessie* (Red Fox)
Ted Hughes, *The Iron Man* (Faber)

9–11

Alan Garner, *Elidor* (Collins)
Alan Gibbons, *The Edge* (Orion)
Alan Temperley, *Harry and the Wrinklies* (Scholastic)
Anne Fine, *Goggle Eyes* (Hamish Hamilton)
Anne Fine, *The Road of Bones* (Corgi))
Anthony Horowitz, *Stormbreaker* (Walker)
Berlie Doherty, *Abela* (Andersen Press)
Beverley Naidoo, *The Other Side of Truth* (Puffin)
Celia Rees, *Witch Child* (Bloomsbury)
Cornelia Funke, *The Thief Lord* (Chicken House)
Daniel Pennac, *The Eye of the Wolf* (Walker)
David Almond, *Skellig* (Hodder)
Eva Ibbotson, *Journey to the River Sea* (Macmillan)
Frank Cottrell Boyce, *Millions* (Macmillan)
Gennifer Choldenko, *Al Capone Does My Shirts* (Bloomsbury)
Geraldine McCaughrean, *The White Darkness* (Oxford)
Gillian Cross, *Wolf* (Oxford)
Henrietta Branford, *Fire, Bed and Bone* (Walker)
Hilary McKay, *Saffy's Angel* (Hodder)
J.K. Rowling, *Harry Potter and the Philosopher's Stone* (Bloomsbury)
Jacqueline Wilson, *Midnight* (Doubleday)
Jacqueline Wilson, *The Illustrated Mum* (Transworld)
Jan Mark, *Thunder and Lightnings* (Kestrel)
Jenny Nimmo, *Children of the Red King: Midnight for Charlie Bone* (Egmont)

Katherine Paterson, *Bridge to Terabithia* (Puffin)
Lemony Snicket, *A Series of Unfortunate Events: The Bad Beginning* (Egmont)
Mal Peet, *Keeper* (Walker)
Malorie Blackman, *Pig Heart Boy* (Doubleday)
Marcus Sedgwick, *The Book of Dead Days* (Orion)
Maurice Gleitzman, *Bumface* (Puffin)
Maurice Gleitzman, *Toad Rage* (Puffin)
Maurice Gleitzman, *Two Weeks with the Queen* (Puffin)
Michael Morpurgo, *Kensuke's Kingdom* (Mammoth)
Michael Morpurgo, *Private Peaceful* (HarperCollins)
Michelle Magorian, *Goodnight Mr Tom* (Longman)
Michelle Paver, *Wolf Brother* (Orion)
Natalie Babbitt, *Tuck Everlasting* (Bloomsbury)
Nicholas Fisk, *A Rag, a Bone and a Hank of Hair* (Kestrel)
Nicky Singer, *Feather Boy* (Collins)
Nina Bawden, *Carrie's War* (Puffin)
Philip Pullman, *Clockwork or All Wound Up* (Doubleday)
Philip Pullman, *Northern Lights* (Scholastic)
Philip Reeve, *Mortal Engines* (Scholastic)
Philip Ridley, *Krindlekrax* (Puffin)
Philippa Pearce, *Tom's Midnight Garden* (Puffin)
Reinhardt Jung, translated by Anthea Bell, *Bambert's Book of Missing Stories* (Egmont)
Roald Dahl, *Matilda* (Puffin)
Robert Westall, *Gulf* (Mammoth)
Russell Hoban, *The Mouse and his Child* (Faber)
Sharon Creech, *Ruby Holler* (Bloomsbury)
Terry Pratchett, *The Amazing Maurice and His Educated Rodents* (Corgi)
William Nicholson, *The Wind Singer* (Mammoth)

Poetry

5-7

Single poet collections

Charles Causley, *Early in the Morning* (Kestrel)
Colin McNaughton, *I'm Talking Big!* (Walker)
Colin McNaughton, *Making Friends with Frankenstein* (Walker)
Giles Andreae, *Commotion in the Ocean* (Orchard)
James Carter, *Hey, Little Bug: Poems for Little Creatures* (Hands Up Books)
John Agard, *Grandfather's Old Bruk-a-Down Car* (Bodley Head)
John Foster, *Bare Bear* (Oxford)
John Foster, *You Little Monkey!* (Oxford)
Judith Nicholls, *Popcorn Pie* (Mary Glasgow Publications)
Roger McGough, *An Imaginary Menagerie* (Puffin)

Tony Mitton, *Fluff and other stuff* (Orchard)
Tony Mitton, *Pip* (Scholastic)
Wendy Cope, *Twiddling Your Thumbs* (Faber)

Anthologies

Fiona Waters, (ed.) *Time for a Rhyme* (Orion)
Jill Bennett, (ed.) *Noisy Poems* (Oxford)
Jill Bennett, (ed.) *Tasty Poems* (Oxford)
Joan Paulson, (ed.) *Sling a Jammy Doughnut* (Wayland)
John Agard and Grace Nichols, (eds) *No Hickory, No Dickory, No Dock* (Puffin)
John Foster, (ed.) *A Red Poetry Paintbox* (Oxford)
John Foster, (ed.) *Cockadoodle Moo* (Oxford)
John Foster, (ed.) *Twinkle, Twinkle Chocolate Bar* (Oxford)
John Foster, (ed.) *Whizz Bang Orang-utan* (Oxford)
John Foster, (ed.) *See You Later, Escalator* (Oxford)
June Crebbin, (ed.) *The Puffin Book of Fantastic First Poems* (Puffin)
Margaret Mayo, (ed.) *Hoddley Poddley: Favourite Rhymes and Verse* (Orchard)
Michael Rosen, (ed.) *Walking the Bridge of your Nose* (Kingfisher)
Pie Corbett, (ed.) *The King's Pyjamas* (Belitha Press)

7–9

Single poet collections

Adrian Henri, *The World's Your Lobster* (Bloomsbury)
Allan Ahlberg, *Friendly Matches* (Viking)
Allan Ahlberg, *Heard It in the Playground* (Viking)
Allan Ahlberg, *Please Mrs Butler* (Viking)
Brian Patten, *Gargling with Jelly* (Puffin)
Brian Patten, *The Utter Nutters* (Viking)
Grace Nichols, *Come On into My Tropical Garden* (A&C Black)
James Carter, *Time-Travelling Underpants* (Macmillan)
June Crebbin, *The Jungle Sale* (Viking)
Kit Wright, *Cat among the Pigeons* (Viking)
Michael Rosen, *Mind Your Own Business* (Andre Deutsch)
Michael Rosen, *Mustard, Custard, Grumble Belly and Gravy* (Bloomsbury)
Peter Dixon, *Grand Prix of Poetry* (Macmillan)
Richard Edwards, *The Very Best of Richard Edwards* (Macmillan)
Roald Dahl, *Songs and Verse* (Cape)
Steve Turner, *Dad, You're Not Funny* (Lion)
Steve Turner, *The Day I Fell Down the Toilet and other poems* (Lion)
Ted Hughes, *The Mermaid's Purse* (Faber)
Tony Mitton, *Big Bad Raps* (Orchard)
Tony Mitton, *Plum* (Scholastic)
Tony Mitton, *The Red and White Spotted Handkerchief* (Scholastic)
Valerie Bloom, *Let Me Touch the Sky: Selected Poems* (Macmillan)

Anthologies

Brian Moses, (ed.) *The Secret Lives of Teachers* (Macmillan)
Brian Patten, (ed.) *The Puffin Book of Utterly Brilliant Poetry* (Viking)
Gerard Benson, (ed.) *Does W Trouble You?* (Puffin)
Jill Bennett, (ed.) *Peace Begins with Me* (Oxford)
John Agard and Grace Nichols, (eds) *A Caribbean Dozen* (Walker)
John Foster, (ed.) *Fantastic Football Poems* (Oxford)
John Foster, (ed.) *Word Whirls* (Oxford)
Kaye Webb, (ed.) *I Like This Poem* (Puffin)
Paul Cookson, (ed.) *The Works* (Macmillan)
Quentin Blake, (ed.) *The Quentin Blake Book of Nonsense Verse* (Viking)
Sarah Garland, (ed.) *Shimmy with my Granny* (Macmillan)
Wes Magee, (ed.) *Madtail, Miniwhale and other shape poems* (Puffin)

9–11

Single poet collections

Benjamin Zephaniah, *Talking Turkeys* (Viking)
Benjamin Zephaniah, *Wicked World* (Puffin)
Carol Ann Duffy, *Meeting Midnight* (Faber)
Carol Ann Duffy, *The Hat* (Faber)
Carol Ann Duffy, *The Oldest Girl in the World* (Faber)
Charles Causley, *Collected Poems for Children* (Macmillan)
Gareth Owen, *Collected Poems for Children* (Macmillan)
Gina Douthwaite, *Picture a Poem: A Book of Shape Poems* (Red Fox)
Helen Dunmore, *Snollygoster and other poems* (Scholastic)
Jackie Kay, *Two's Company* (Blackie)
James Carter, *Cars, Stars, Electric Guitars* (Walker)
Lindsay MacRae, *How to Avoid Kissing Your Parents in Public* (Puffin)
Philip Gross, *Scratch City* (Faber)
Philip Gross, *The All-Nite Café* (Faber)
Roger McGough, *All the Best: Selected Poems* (Puffin)
Russell Hoban, *The Last of the Wallendas and other poems* (Hodder)
Sharon Creech, *Love That Dog* (Bloomsbury)
Ted Hughes, *Collected Poems for Children* (Faber)

Anthologies

Adrian Mitchell, (ed.) *The Thirteen Secrets of Poetry* (Simon and Schuster)
Anne Harvey, (ed.) *He Said, She Said, They Said* (Blackie)
Anne Harvey, (ed.) *Shades of Green* (Julia MacRae)
Fiona Waters, (ed.) *The Poetry Book* (Orion)
Fiona Waters, (ed.) *Glitter When You Jump* (Macmillan)
Gerard Benson, (ed.) *This Poem Doesn't Rhyme* (Puffin)
Grace Nichols, (ed.) *Can I Buy a Slice of Sky?* (Blackie)

James Berry, (ed.) *Classic Poems to Read Aloud* (Kingfisher)
James Carter, (ed.) *Rap It Up* (Questions Publishing)
John Agard and Grace Nichols, (eds) *Under the Moon and Over the Sea* (Walker)
John Agard, (ed.) *Why Is the Sky?* (Faber)
John Foster, (ed.) *Crack Another Yolk* (Oxford)
John Foster, (ed.) *101 Favourite Poems: Poets Pick Their Favourite Poem* (Collins)
Judith Nicholls, (ed.) *Wordspells* (Faber)
Julie Johnstone, (ed.) *The Thing that Mattered Most: Scottish Poems for Children* (Black and White Publishing)
Michael Rosen, (ed.) *A World of Poetry* (Kingfisher)
Michael Rosen, (ed.) *Classic Poetry: An Illustrated Collection* (Walker)
Roger McGough, (ed.) *Strictly Private* (Viking)
Roger McGough, (ed.) *Sensational: Poems Inspired by the Five Senses* (Macmillan)
Tony Medina, *(ed.) Love to Langston* (Lee and Low Books)
Véronique Tadjo, (ed.) *Talking Drums* (A&C Black)

Useful Sources of Information about Children's Books, Authors and Reading

Books

Booktrust, *The Best Book Guide for Children and Young Adults:*   Guide produced annually, presenting its choice of the best new paperback fiction for all ages across a variety of genres and subjects (download from www.booktrust.org.uk).

CLPE, *Book Power: Literacy through Literature* (Centre for Literacy in Primary Education, Webber Street, London, SE1 8QW):   A series of practical guides each of which features ten powerful books to create a literature programme for different year groups in the primary school.

CLPE, *Simply the Best Books for Children: Books for 0–7 years* and *Simply the Best Books for Children: Books for 7–11 years* (Centre for Literacy in Primary Education, Webber Street, London, SE1 8QW):   Annotated booklists aimed at parents and designed to help foster children's enjoyment of reading and books.

CLPE, *The Core Book List* (Centre for Literacy in Primary Education, Webber Street, London, SE1 8QW):   A comprehensive, annotated booklist for primary teachers. The booklist is made up of three main collections, Learning to Read, the Literature Collection and the Information Book Collection. The list is updated every two years.

Daniel Hahn and Leonie Flynn, *The Ultimate Book Guide* (A&C Black):   A single-volume guide which lists more than 600 books for 8–12-year-old readers and provides reviews by children's authors, editors and children themselves.

Edgardo Zaghini and Deborah Hallford, *Outside In: Children's Books in Translation* (Milet Publishing): A guide to children's books translated into English, for parents, teachers, librarians and other professionals, containing articles, reviews, a resource guide, and biographies of writers, illustrators and translators.

Edgardo Zaghini and Deborah Hallford, *Universal Verse: Poetry for Children* (Barn Owl Books): An extensive guide for parents, teachers, librarians and other professionals to currently available poetry books for children.

Jacqueline Wilson (introduced by) *Great Book to Read Aloud,* (Corgi): A guide for parents to over 70 'tried and tested' read alouds for children from 0 to11 years, with tips from experts, recommendations from celebrity parents and sample extracts (see also www.greatbookstoreadaloud.co.uk).

Nicholas Tucker, *Rough Guide to Children's Books: Under 5 Years* (Rough Guides): Gives details of over 140 recommended books for very young children, organised by age and subject matter, including reviews, synopses and evaluations.

Nicholas Tucker, *Rough Guide to Children's Books: 5–11 Years* (Rough Guides): Gives details of recommended books for KS1 and KS2 children, ranging from picture books to novels and poetry, and organised by age and subject matter, including reviews, synopses and evaluations of educational potential.

Norah Irvin and Lesley Cooper, *Who Next ...?: A Guide to Children's Authors* (2nd edn, Library and Information Statistics Unit): For each of the 400+ children's writers listed, other authors who write in a similar way are listed as suggestions for 'who to read next'. The book is organised by age groups: 5–7, 8–11 and 12–14. It also includes information on picture books for older readers, an index of authors by genre, a list of children's book series, and a list of award winners.

Paul B. Janeczko, illustrated by Paul Raschka, *A Kick in the Head: An Everyday Guide to Poetic Forms* (Walker): A lively and imaginative text that can be enjoyed in many ways – as a superbly illustrated anthology, a comprehensive reference guide and a stimulus for writing in a wide range of formats.

Periodicals

Armadillo: An independent quarterly periodical with reviews and articles, often by leading children's writers. Founded and managed by the mother and daughter team of Mary Hoffman and Rhiannon Lassiter, both well-known children's authors. (www.armadillomagazine.com)

Books for Keeps: An independent magazine published every two months with news, reviews, editorial, letters page, articles and regular features about children's books and reading. (www.booksforkeeps.co.uk)

Book Trusted: Magazine of Booktrust, an independent national charity which encourages enjoyment of reading for all ages and cultures, containing news about book events, interviews with children's authors, extensive lists of recommended books for different age groups, and teachers' resources. (www. booktrusted.co.uk)

Carousel: A quarterly magazine published by the Federation of Children's Book Groups, containing reviews, articles and features on and by contemporary children's authors. (www.carouselguide.co.uk)

School Librarian: Quarterly journal of the School Library Association, containing news about the children's book world, extensive reviews of new books, and articles about reading and libraries. (www.sla.org.uk/school-librarian.php)

Websites

www.achuka.co.uk   A child-friendly independent website edited by primary teacher Michael Thorn, which offers reviews, news and features about children's books, as well as a facility to purchase them online. There is also a database of picture books, searchable by keywords.

www.bigpicture.org.uk   A site to promote picture books, run by Booktrust, and aimed at all those interested in the genre, including teachers and students, containing downloadable guides, author information, news about events and other resources.

www.bookmark.org.uk   Another Booktrust-run website, which offers news, advice, information and resources related to disability issues and children's books.

www.channel4learning.net/sites/bookbox   A child-friendly website linked to the popular Channel 4 schools programme *Book Box*, which offers interviews with and information about over 30 popular children's novelists, poets and picture book authors. It includes video clips of interviews with writers, along with games and other interactive features.

www.childrenslaureate.org.uk   The official website which offers news and information about the current Children's Laureate and previous authors who have carried out the role. It is aimed primarily at adults, with a section for teachers.

www.childrenspoetrybookshelf.co.uk   The Children's Poetry Bookshelf was set up as a book club by the Poetry Book Society with the aim of encouraging children to read, write and enjoy poetry. The website is aimed at children and, as well as poems, offers book reviews, competitions and 'fun stuff'. There is an adult section for teachers, parents and librarians with guidance on encouraging children to enjoy poetry.

www.classicalcomics.com   A UK site offering graphic novel adaptations of classic literature, including Shakespeare and Dickens, suitable for older primary children and promoted as attractive to boys and reluctant readers in particular. The Shakespeare plays offer a choice of the unabridged original text, a modernised 'plain text' version, and a simplified 'Quick Text' version.

www.comicsintheclassroom.net   A Canadian website covering all types of comics and how they can be used in school, with lesson plans, news, reviews, features and a kids' blog.

www.cool-reads.co.uk   On this site, books for 10–15-year-old readers are reviewed by 10–15-year-old reviewers, in various categories of genre and theme. The site was originally founded by two boys, Chris and Tim, when they were themselves 10–15-year-olds.

www.geocities.com/talestoldtall   A US website for adults run by Michael Sullivan, storyteller and children's author. It has a clear educational emphasis and includes articles and books for educators about getting boys reading.

www.guysread.com   The author Jon Szceiska's site for children and young adults, which is dedicated to encouraging boys to read. Slightly anarchic and deliberately non-educational in approach, it has book recommendations, though mostly of US titles, and includes a search facility.

www.kidsreview.org.uk   This site contains thousands of book reviews produced at school and at home by children of all ages for other children There are also details of books available online and useful information about the favourite children's books of well-known authors and sportsmen. Some parts are free, others require subscription.

www.lovereading4schools.co.uk   This site provides annotated book lists with information about authors for each year from Y1 to Y9 for teachers and parents. There is also the facility to buy the books at discounted prices. Schools and parents have to register to access lists but the site is then free to use.

www.myhomelibrary.org   Inspired by the former Children's Laureate Anne Fine, this site offers children and young adults the opportunity to download or create bookplates and bookmarks, as well as read book reviews by Anne Fine herself and by children.

www.openingthebook.com   A British website supporting library development and reader development in all its aspects.

www.poetryarchive.org/childrensarchive   This area of the wonderful Poetry Archive website has child-friendly pages containing information about children's poets and also video clips of them being interviewed and reading their work. The pages are searchable by theme, poetic form, or poet. CDs of the readings can be ordered online.

www.poetryclass.net   Maintained by the Poetry Society, this site aims to take the fear out of teaching poetry and promote enjoyment for teachers and pupils. There is free access to resources, lesson plans and interviews with poets, and in-service training and visits to schools by poets are offered.

www.poetryzone.ndirect.co.uk   A child-oriented poetry website edited by children's poet Roger Stevens, containing reviews and interviews as well as poems for and by children. There is also a Teacher Zone with classroom resources and information.

www.readingmatters.co.uk   Edited by Jill Marshall for 'intelligent young readers who are keen to choose their own books', this site offers reviews and articles for children and teenagers about the ideas behind books, particularly new ones, without recourse to 'dumbing down'.

www.smartgirl.org   Another US site, this time aimed at teenage girls, which covers a host of topics, including reading. It contains book reviews by children and young adults, and useful surveys of teenage reading habits, although these do not claim to be scientific.

www.storiesfromtheweb.org.uk   This site is part of a reader development programme for libraries run by Birmingham Libraries. Its stated aim is to promote a love of reading and to encourage creative reading and writing activities. There are child-friendly web pages with adult sections, and the site is free to use, though schools have to subscribe to publish reviews on the site.

www.storybookengland.com   An interactive map of places connected with children's authors produced by the Enjoy England tourist authority.

www.storyquest.org.uk   This site gives details of a regular UK national festival of storytelling and the spoken word aimed at families and children, sponsored by the Prince's Foundation for Children and the Arts.

www.writeaway.org.uk   This is a free online children's book resource for teachers, students and librarians, edited by lecturer, writer and in-service training provider Nikki Gamble. The site contains interviews, resources, reading suggestions connected to popular themes and issues, and reviews of children's books for KS1–3.

www.writingtogether.org.uk   A site run by Booktrust offering information and step-by-step advice for teachers on organising author visits to school, including case studies.

Audio Books

www.audible.co.uk   A website offering audio files which are downloadable to PCs, iPods and other devices.

www.audiobookcollection.com   A website that specialises in unabridged recordings on tape and CD by well-known readers, including the BBC radio collection, the Puffin and Penguin catalogues, and the Naxos library.

www.bags-of-books.co.uk   An independent children's bookshop specialising in spoken word tapes and CDs.

www.bbcaudiobooks.com   This site includes the previous catalogues of Chivers and Cover to Cover, as well as the BBC's own unrivalled collection.

www.talkingbooks.co.uk   A bookshop which deals exclusively in audio books on tape, CD or MP3CD.

Children's Magazines and Newspapers

www.aquila.co.uk   A children's magazine aimed at able 8–13-year-olds. Each issue has an overall topic or theme, and includes a story.

www.boox.org.uk   A magazine promoting books and reading, produced by teenagers for teenagers.

www.firstnews.co.uk   A children's tabloid newspaper, available in print and online.

www.thenewspaper.org.uk   A children's broadsheet newspaper, available in print and online.

Useful Organisations that Promote Reading for Pleasure

www.bookaid.org   A website dedicated to developing global literacy through charitable donations. There is a Kid Zone where children can explore the global dimension of reading and discover how they can help spread the pleasures of reading to children in developing countries. There are also teacher resources for World Book Day and booklists of multicultural reading.

www.clpe.co.uk/powerofreading   The aims of the CLPE Power of Reading Project are 'to enhance children's pleasure in reading and to raise children's achievement through teachers' knowledge of literature and its use in the classroom'. The project began in 2005–6 with 50 teachers and 2000 children in 30 schools and 12 local authorities.

www.educationguardian.co.uk/conferences   This site gives details of occasional Reading for Pleasure conferences which are provided for primary and secondary schools.

www.fcbg.org.uk   Website of the Federation of Children's Book Groups, a voluntary organisation which coordinates the activities of parents' book groups across the country. Its aim is to promote enthusiasm for children's books through group meetings, author visits and other book events involving parents and children. The Federation organises the Red House Children's Book Award, the National Share-a-Story Month in May and publishes the magazine *Carousel*.

www.literacytrust.org.uk   This superb website should be the first stop for anyone interested in promoting reading. Amongst many other things, it provides links to

- *Reading Connects:* trying to build a network of schools that promote reading
- *Reading Champions:* encouraging male readers to act as role models for boys
- *Reading the Game*: working with footballers to promote reading motivation
- *National Year of Reading*: information on the NYR for 2008

www.ncll.org.uk   The website of the National Centre for Language and Literacy based at the University of Reading offers teachers free searchable databases of children's books, teacher resources and authors who are available to visit schools. There are also recommended books of different types for different age groups and information about NCLL publications for teachers and parents, which can be ordered online. Additional resources are available to subscribing members.

www.readathon.org   The official site which provides free materials to support teachers holding reading marathons to raise money for charitable causes.

www.roalddahlmuseum.org   Website of the Roald Dahl Museum and Story Centre. This gives information for parents and schools about the Centre and how to visit it. There is also a searchable archive of material such as story drafts, photographs and artefacts related to Dahl held by the Centre, which is suitable for children to use and includes a virtual tour of his former writing hut.

www.sevenstories.org.uk   Website of the Centre for Children's Books based in Newcastle, which provides information about the only exhibition space dedicated to British children's literature in the United Kingdom.

www.sla.org.uk   The School Library Association website. The SLA supports all those involved in school libraries, whether primary or secondary, with the aim of developing effective school library provision for every pupil. It runs the government's 'Boys into Books' scheme and publishes the journal *School Librarian*, which contains library and children's book news as well as extensive book reviews.

Useful Books on Promoting Reading for Pleasure

Claire Senior, *Getting the Buggers to Read* (Continuum, 2005):   A guide for secondary school teachers which addresses the questions 'Why is reading important?', 'How can I motivate my students to read?' and 'How can I make reading fun?', with practical suggestions, examples and recommended reading lists.

Paul Jennings, *The Reading Bug ... and how you can help your child to catch it* (Penguin, 2004):   A practical guide for parents offering strategies for helping children learn to love books, including suggestions for reading for primary and secondary age children, written by a popular Australian children's writer.

Reading Connects, *Creating a Reading Culture Handbook: Primary* (DfES): Freely downloadable from www.readingconnects.org.uk, this is a booklet produced for primary schools that have joined the Reading Connects network, giving extensive advice and practical tips for promoting reading at whole school level from experts in the field, such as Prue Goodwin.

References

Allan, J., Ellis, S. and Pearson, C. (2005) *Literature Circles, Gender and Reading for Enjoyment*. Edinburgh: Scottish Executive Education Department (www.scotland.gov.uk/Publications/2005/11/SRLitCir)

Almond, D. (1998) *Skellig*. London: Hodder

Almond, D. (1999) *Kit's Wilderness*. London: Hodder

Armitage, R. and Armitage, D. (1977) *The Lighthouse Keeper's Lunch*. London: Andre Deutsch

Arts Council (2003) From Looking Glass to Spyglass. London: Arts Council England

Ashley, B., Blake, Q., Fine, A., Gavin, J., Morpurgo, M., Powling, C., Prince, A., Pullman, P., Rosen, M. and Wilson, J. (2005) *Waiting for a Jamie Oliver: Beyond Bog-standard Literacy*. University of Reading: National Centre for Language and Literacy

Baddeley, P. and Eddershaw, C. (1994) *Not So Simple Picture Books: Developing Responses to Literature with 4–12 Year Olds*. Stoke-on-Trent: Trentham Books

Baker, L. and Wigfield, A. (1999) 'Dimensions of children's motivation for reading and their relations to reading activity and reading achievement', *Reading Research Quarterly*, 34 (4), 452–476

Baker, L., Scher, D. and Mackler, K. (1997) 'Home and family influences on motivations for readings', *Educational Psychologist*, 32, 69–82

Barrs, M. and Pidgeon, S. (eds) (1993) *Reading the Difference: Gender and Reading in the Primary School*. London: Centre for Literacy in Primary Education

Barrs, M. and Pidgeon, S. (1998) *Boys and Reading*. London: Centre for Literacy in Primary Education

Bell, D. (2005) Speech for World Book Day, March (www.ofsted.gov.uk)

Benton, M. and Fox, G. (1985) *Teaching Literature 9–14*. Oxford: Oxford University Press

Bishop, Z. (2006) *Times Educational Supplement*, 1 December

Bleach, K. (ed.) (1998) *Raising Boys' Achievement in Schools*. Stoke-on-Trent: Trentham Books

Bloom, A. and Marley, D. (2007) *Times Educational Supplement*, 1 June

Bostock, M. (1993) *Think of an Eel*. London: Walker Books

Briggs, R. (1982) *When the Wind Blows*. London: Hamish Hamilton

Briggs, R. (1984) *The Tin-Pot Foreign General and the Old Iron Woman*. London: Hamish Hamilton

Brown, R. (1981) *A Dark, Dark Tale*. London: Andersen Press

Browne, A. (1979) *Bear Hunt*. London: Hamish Hamilton

Browne, A. (1981) *Hansel and Gretel*. London: Julia MacRae

Browne, A. (1983) *Gorilla*. London: Julia MacRae

Browne, A. (1984) *Willy the Wimp*. London: Julia MacRae

Browne, A. (1986) *Piggybook*. London: Julia MacRae

Browne, A. (1998) *Voices in the Park*. London: Doubleday

Bruner, J. (1996) *The Culture of Education*. Cambridge, MA: Harvard University Press

Burningham, J. (1977) *Come Away from the Water, Shirley*. London: Cape

Burningham, J. (1978) *Would You Rather...* London: Cape

Burningham, J. (1984) *Granpa*. London: Cape

Burningham, J. (1986) *Where's Julius?* London: Cape

Carter, J. (2007) 'Whatever happened to children's poetry?', *Carousel*, 35, 14–15

Celebrating Reading Connects magazine, December 2005 (www.literacytrust.org.uk/campaign/Celebrating_Reading_Connects)

Chambers, A. (1969) *The Reluctant Reader*. Oxford: Pergamon Press

Chambers, A. (1973) *Introducing Books to Children*. London: Heinemann Educational Books

Chambers, A. (1993) 'The difference of literature: writing now for the future of young readers', *Children's Literature in Education*, 24, 1

Cox, B. (ed.) (1998) *Literacy Is Not Enough: Essays on the Importance of Reading*. Manchester: Manchester University Press and Book Trust

Craig, P. (2006) 'Katie Morag Days', *English 4–11*, 28, 19–20

Cremin, T., Bearne, E., Goodwin, P. and Mottram, M. (2007) 'Teachers as readers', *English 4–11*, No. 30 (Summer)

Cunningham, A.E. and Stanovich, K.E. (1998) 'What reading does for the mind', *American Educator* 22 (1&2), 8–15

Daily Telegraph (2003) 'Forget the namby-pamby girly stuff, here are ripping yarns for real chaps', 10 October

DfEE/QCA (1999) *The National Curriculum: Handbook for Primary Teachers in England*. London: HMSO

DfES (2003) *Excellence and Enjoyment: A Strategy for Primary Schools*. London: DfES

DfES (2005) *Raising Standards in Reading: Achieving Children's Targets*. London: DfES

DfES (2006a) *Primary Framework for Literacy and Mathematics*. London: DfES

DfES (2006b) *Independent Review of the Teaching of Early Reading* (The Rose Review). London: DfES (www.standards.dfes.gov.uk/phonics/report.pdf)

DfES (2007a) *Letters and Sounds: Principles and Practice of High Quality Phonics*. London: DfES

DfES (2007b) *Practice Guidance for the Early Years Foundation Stage*. London: DfES

DfES (2007c) *Statutory Framework for the Early Years Foundation Stage*. London: DfES

Donaldson, J. and Scheffler, A. (1999) *The Gruffalo*. London: Macmillan

Dungworth, N., Grimshaw, S., McKnight, C. and Morris, A. (2004) 'Reading for pleasure?: A summary of the findings from a survey of the reading habits of Year 5 pupils', *New Review of Children's Literature and Librarianship*, 10 (2), 169–188

Elkin, J., Train, B. and Denhan, D. (2003) *Reading and Reader Development: The Pleasure of Reading*. London: Facet

Fine, A. (1989) *Bill's New Frock*. London: Methuen

Fine, A. (1992) *Flour Babies*. London: Hamish Hamilton

Foreman, M. (1997) *War Game*. London: Pavilion Books

French, F. (1986) *Snow White in New York*. Oxford: Oxford University Press

Funke, C. (trans. O. Latsch) (2003) *The Thief Lord*. Frome, Somerset: The Chicken House

Gambrell, L.B. and Marinak, B. (1997) 'Incentive and intrinsic motivation to read', in J.Guthrie and A. Wigfield (eds), Reading Engagement: Motivating Readers Through Integrated Instruction. Newark, DE: International Reading Association

Gambrell, L.B. (1996) 'Creating classroom cultures that foster motivation', *The Reading Teacher*, 50 (1), 14–25

Gambrell, L.B., Palmer, B.M., Codling, R.M. and Mazzoni, S.A. (1996) 'Assessing motivation to read', *The Reading Teacher*, 49 (7), 518–533

Gavin, J. (1994) *Grandpa Chatterji*. London: Mammoth

Grahame, K. (1908) *The Wind in the Willows*. London: Methuen

Guthrie, J., Van Meter, P., McCann, A.,Wigfield, A., Bennett, L., Poundstone, C., Rice, M.E., Faibisch, F.M., Hunt, B. and Mitchell, A.M. (1996) 'Growth of literacy engagement: changes in motivations and strategies during concept-oriented reading instruction', *Reading Research Quarterly*, 31 (3), 306–331

Hall, C. and Coles, M. (1999) *Children's Reading Choices*. London: Routledge

Hathorn, L. and Rogers, G. (2003) *Way Home*. London: Andersen Press

Hedderwick, M. (1995) *Katie Morag and the Wedding*. London: Bodley Head

Henry, J. (2007) 'Reading is for the "nerds", say children', *Sunday Telegraph*, 11 March

Hilton, M. (2007) 'Measuring standards in primary English: issues of validity and accountability with respect to PIRLS and National Curriculum test scores', *British Educational Research Journal*, 32 (6), 817–837

Hoban, R. and Blake, Q. (1974) *How Tom Beat Captain Najork and His Hired Sportsmen*. London: Cape

Hoffman, M. and Binch, C. (1991) *Amazing Grace*. London: Frances Lincoln

Hoffman, M. and Littlewood, K. (2002) *The Colour of Home*. London: Frances Lincoln

Horowitz, A. (2000) *Stormbreaker*. London: Walker Books

House of Commons Education and Skills Committee (2005) *Teaching Children to Read*. London: The Stationery Office

Hughes, T. (1968) *The Iron Man*. London: Faber

Iggulden, H. and Iggulden, C. (2006) *The Dangerous Book for Boys*. London: HarperCollins

Ingham, J. (1982) *Books and Reading Development: the Bradford Book Flood Experiment*, 2nd edn. Portsmouth, NH: Heinemann

Innocento, R. and McEwan, I. (1985) *Rose Blanche*. London: Cape

International Association for the Evaluation of Educational Achievement (2001) *Progress in International Reading Literacy Study* (www.isc.bc.edu/pirls2001)

Irwin, N. (2003) 'Personal constructs and the enhancement of adolescent engagement in reading', *Support for Learning*, 18 (1), 29–34

Ivey, G. and Broaddus, K. (2001) '"Just Plain Reading?": A survey of what makes students want to read in middle school classrooms', *Reading Research Quarterly*, 36 (4), 350–377

Jung, R. (2002) *Bambert's Book of Missing Stories*. London: Egmont

Krashen, S. (2004) *The Power of Reading: Insights from the Research*, 2nd edn. Westport, CT: Libraries Unlimited

Legg, J. (2006) 'Teachers escape through reading', *Times Educational Supplement*, 22 September

Lewis, D. (1990) 'The constructedness of texts: picture books and the metafictive', *Signal*, 62, 131–146

Lewis, M. and Ellis, S. (eds) (2006) *Phonics: Practice, Research and Policy*. London: PCP/UKLA

Lockwood, M. (1998) 'Developing poetry', in Andrew Goodwyn (ed.), *Literary and Media Texts in Secondary English: New Approaches*. London: Cassell

Lockwood, M. (2007) 'Surveying the pleasures of reading', *NATE Classroom*, 1 (1), 46–48

Magorian, M. (1987) *Goodnight Mr Tom*. London: Puffin Books

Mansell, W. and Ward, H. (2007) 'Don't cram, teach', *Times Educational Supplement*, 10 August

Martin, T. (1989) *The Strugglers*. Buckingham: Open University Press

McKee, D. (1980) *Not Now, Bernard*. London: Andersen Press

McKee, D. (2004) *The Conquerors*. London: Andersen Press

Meek, M. (1991) *On Being Literate*. London: The Bodley Head

Millard, E. (1997) *Differently Literate: Boys, Girls and the Schooling of Literacy*. London: Falmer Press

Miskin, R. (2006–) *Read Write Inc* series. Oxford: Oxford University Press

Morpurgo, M. (1996) *The Butterfly Lion*. London: Collins

Morpurgo, M. (1999) *Kensuke's Kingdom*. London: Egmont

Murphy, J. (1982) *On the Way Home*. London: Macmillan

Museums, Libraries and Archives Council (2005) 'Literature Matters – Raising the profile of children's literature in teacher training'. (www.mla.gov.uk)

National Literacy Trust (2005) *Children's and Young People's Reading Habits and Preferences* (www.literacytrust.org.uk)

National Literacy Trust (2007) *Getting the Blokes on Board* (www.literacytrust.org.uk)

Nell, V. (1988) *Lost In a Book: The Psychology of Reading for Pleasure*. New Haven, CT: Yale University Press

Ofsted (2004) *Reading for Purpose and Pleasure* (www.ofsted.gov.uk)

Ofsted (2005) *English 2000–05: A Review of Inspection Evidence* (www.ofsted.gov.uk)

Ofsted (2006) *Good School Libraries: Making a Difference to Learning* (www.ofsted.gov.uk)

Organisation for Economic Co-operation and Development (OECD) (2002) *Reading for Change: Results from PISA 2000* (www.pisa.oecd.org)

Organisation for Economic Co-operation and Development (OECD) (2007) *PISA 2006: Science Competencies for Tomorrow's World. Volume 1: Analysis. Volume 2: Data* (www.pisa.oecd.org)

Paver, M. (2004–) *Chronicles of Ancient Darkness* series. London: Orion

Pennac, D. (2002) *The Eye of the Wolf.* London: Walker Books

Pennac, D. (2006) *The Rights of the Reader.* London: Walker Books.

Powling, C., Ashley, B., Pullman, P., Fine, A. and Gavin, J. (2003) *Meetings with the Minister: Five Children's Authors on the National Literacy Strategy.* University of Reading: National Centre for Language and Literacy

Pratchett, T. (1993) *The Carpet People.* London: Corgi

QCA (2005) *English 21: Playback.* London: Qualifications and Curriculum Authority

QCA (2006) *Taking English Forward: The Four Cs.* London: Qualifications and Curriculum Authority

Reeve, P. (2001) *Mortal Engines.* London: Scholastic

Roberts, R. (2006) 'Puzzling together: Y6 children thinking and talking in literature circles', *English 4–11,* 28, 17–18

Ross, C.S., McKechnie, L. and Rothbauer, P.M. (2006) *Reading Matters: What Research Reveals about Reading, Libraries and Community.* Westport, CT: Libraries Unlimited

Sainsbury, M. and Schagen, I. (2004) 'Attitudes to reading at ages nine and eleven', *Journal of Research in Reading,* 27 (4), 373–386

Scieszka, J. and Johnson, S. (1994) *The Frog Prince Continued.* London: Puffin Books

Scieszka, J. and Smith, L. (1991) *The True Story of the Three Little Pigs.* London: Puffin Books

Simon, F. (1995) *Horrid Henry.* London: Orion

Smith, J. and Alcock, A. (1990) *Revisiting Literacy.* Buckingham: Open University Press

Spiegel, D. (1981) *Reading for Pleasure: Guidelines.* Newark, DE: International Reading Association

Stewart, P. and Riddell, C. (2004–) *The Edge Chronicles* series. Oxford: David Fickling Books

Swindells, R. (1977) *The Ice Palace.* London: Hamish Hamilton

TES (Times Educational Supplement) (2004) 4 June

TES (Times Educational Supplement) (2007) 30 November

Trivizas, E. and Oxenbury, H. (1993) *The Three Little Wolves and the Big Bad Pig,* London: Heinemann

Turner, J.C. (1997) in J.T. Guthrie & A. Wigfield (eds) *Reading Engagement: motivating readers through integrated instruction.* Newark, DE: International Reading Association

Twist, L., Sainsbury, M., Woodthorpe, A. and Whetton, C. (2003) *Reading All Over the World: PIRLS National Report for England.* Slough: National Foundation for Educational Research

Twist, L., Gnaldi, M., Schagen, I., and Morrison, J. (2004) 'Good readers but at a cost? Attitudes to Reading in England', *Journal of Research in Reading,* 27 (4) 387–400

Van Allsburg, C. (1984) *The Mysteries of Harris Burdick.* Boston, MA: Houghton Mifflin

Varley, S. (1984) *Badger's Parting Gifts.* London: Andersen Press

Wagner, J. and Brooks, R. (1977) *John Brown, Rose and the Midnight Cat.* London: Kestrel

Ward, H. (2007) 'Cornered on poets', *Times Educational Supplement,* 1 June

Wells, G. (1986) *The Meaning Makers: Children Learning Language and Using Language to Learn.* Portsmouth, NH: Heinemann

Willis, J. and Ross, T. (2002) *Dr Xargle's Book of Earthlets.* London: Andersen Press

Wilson, J. (1992) *The Suitcase Kid.* London: Doubleday

Wormell, C. (2003) *Two Frogs.* London: Jonathan Cape

Wyse, D. and Styles, M. (2007) 'Synthetic Phonics and the teaching of reading: the debate surrounding England's "Rose Report"', *Literacy,* 41 (1) 35–42

Index